EVERYTHING YOU EVER WANTED TO KNOW ABOUT THE WORLD CUP

VOLUME THREE:1970-1978

BY SAM BERKELEY

First published in 2014

ISBN 978-1-291-41665-7

By the same author:

Everything You Ever Wanted To Know About the World Cup
Volume One: 1930-1954
Volume Two: 1958-1966
Volume Three: 1970-1978
Volume Four: 1982-1990
Volume Five: 1994-1998
Volume Six: 2002-2006
Volume Seven: 2010-2014 plus All-time World Cup Squads

CONTENTS

Foreword by Gary Lineker   5

Introduction   7

1970 Mexico   9

1974 West Germany   49

1978 Argentina   91

FOREWORD

Playing in the World Cup is the peak of any player's career. Club football might have all the money and might take up the vast majority of the season, but the international game has something domestic football can never match: the ability to unite a country. To put on the national team shirt is what every boy dreams of as a child and in the international game there is nothing that compares to the World Cup.

I was lucky enough in my time as a player to go to two World Cups and I still treasure my experiences in those two tournaments more than any other moments in my footballing career. Of course in 1986 and 1990 there were both fabulous highs and unbearable lows, but that is what football, and in particular the World Cup, is all about. Winning the Golden Boot in '86 and finishing as the highest British goalscorer in World Cup history are records I treasure; but at the same time no moments haunt me like Maradona's two goals and that heartbreaking penalty shoot-out loss to the Germans four years later. To play in the World Cup is to go through a rollercoaster of emotions, just as is watching it on TV. Because it matters so much, because you know an entire country is urging you, begging you to win, that is why the World Cup remains the world's most popular sporting tournament.

The World Cup has made generation after generation fall in love with football. Even those who aren't footie fans the rest of the time can't help but be captivated by the gladiatorial spectacle which takes over the black box in the corner of every home every four years. Millions around the world will watch and wish they were on the pitch themselves. Only a tiny handful will ever achieve that lofty ambition, but those that do will have been inspired by those childhood dreams.

For the vast majority for whom playing in the competition forever remains a pipedream, they must find another way to get their World Cup fix. Watching game after game on TV, absorbing trivia and endlessly talking about the tournament to anyone who'll listen are just some of the ways a World Cup obsessed fan can maximise their own enjoyment of the competition. And of course when it comes to books there are a large number for the World Cup lover to choose from.

Most World Cup books fall into two categories: the encyclopaedia types full of facts and stats; and the passing guides, which give a general overview of the World Cup. There's little in between the two, nothing which gives the reader all the information in an accessible and entertaining way, nothing both comprehensive and easily readable.

Where this series of books delivers, and others fail, is in that middle ground. Each volume is packed full of all the facts and figures even the most ardent World Cup fan could ever need, with not a single game, in qualifying or the finals, ignored. From 1930 to 2010 every tournament is covered in the utmost detail. But it can also be picked up and enjoyed by someone with just a passing interest in the game, with interesting trivia – and some of the bizarre incidents which make the World Cup so special – highlighted to make it easier for the reader to get to the heart of the most interesting bits of each tournament.

Over the years, some of the greatest footballers to have ever played the game have graced the World Cup and given career-defining performances. No-one who ever saw them could forget Diego Maradona's mesmerizing displays in 1986, Pele's masterclass in 1970, or Ronaldo's predatory finishing in 2002. These legends are far from forgotten in this series too, featuring as it does brief biographies of some of the World Cup's all-time greatest players (from Jose Nasazzi to Carles Puyol, Gerd Muller to yours truly!) There's also a personal touch provided from the author, Sam Berkeley, with the selection of some personal all-time teams for the tournament's most successful nations. Debates over great players and teams can go on forever and these selections are sure to add plenty more fuel to the fire!

Even if the football in more recent tournaments hasn't always been of the highest standard, there is no doubt at all that the World Cup will still be holding millions around the world in its spell for decades to come. No matter what happens, football fans will always treasure it and count down the months and years before it is upon them once again. With this series of books you can make sure you're always prepared for and excited about the next instalment. And with your appetite whetted, the football itself will be even more enjoyable.

The World Cup has been a glorious crowd-pleaser for close on a century now. Long may it continue to be the pinnacle of every player's career. Here's to the next 100 years.

Gary Lineker

Introduction

"WHAT THE HELL WERE YOU THINKING?!" The living room exploded in a burst of fury as profanities were spat out and fingers jabbed in the direction of the little black box in the corner. "PLEASE DON'T SEND HIM OFF, PLEASE!" But it was too late. With an icy, emotionless stare the referee reached into the pocket of his garish red neon shirt and out came a flash of scarlet. Time seemed to slow down as realisation slowly dawned on the small semicircle enclosing the television. That was that. There was no hope. England were surely dead and buried now. David Beckham, my hero just a game before, was now the arch-villain of the household.

For me, the World Cup has always been the ultimate. As great as club football is, for all the thrills and spills of the Premiership, La Liga and the Champions League, nothing can touch the sheer passion and importance of the international game. Somehow when the pride of an entire nation is at stake, winning becomes so much more than a priority; it becomes a necessity. As a fresh-faced 11-year-old, France 98 captured my imagination in a way football had never done before. Religiously following England, I cheered against Tunisia, cried against Romania and was left with a strange mix of pride, rage and utter desolation after that Argentina game, Beckham's red card and penalty heartache. The world's most popular sporting competition has kept me held firmly in its grip ever since.

What makes the World Cup so great is all the subplots running through every fixture, from the earliest preliminaries in qualifying all the way to the final itself. The varying hopes and expectations of the contestants are all the more important when these contestants represent countries, where defeat can plunge a state into depression (and in the case of Argentina in 1930 even prompt a revolution!) and victory can revive an entire nation. For some it is merely the taking part that counts, for others anything but the trophy is a tragedy. The format allows for all sorts of intriguing possibilities. What happens when two weaker teams meet each other and have the rare chance of victory? What about when two of the games' giants clash and for both victory is not just clamoured for but demanded? And what about when the Davids meet the Goliaths and the intriguing possiblity of a monumental upset rears its head?

The World Cup is full of these intriguing storylines, every time throwing up results and events which even a fairytale writer would reject as too fanciful. Who would possibly have predicted that North Korea would beat Italy in 1966? That reigning champions France would not score a single goal in 2002? That a particularly bad-tempered qualifier in 1969 would prompt a full-scale war between Honduras and El Salvador? The World Cup captures the hearts and minds of people the world over precisely because it is so unpredictable and intriguing.

But more than anything else the World Cup is the pinnacle of football because it provides a nation with hopes and dreams of glory every four years. Through the good times and the bad the memories are surely the most vivid in football, be they the glory of 1966's triumph or the sorrow of 1990's penalty agony; Michael Owen's 1998 wonder goal against Argentina or Diego Maradona's own masterpiece for the other side back in 1986. Every country treasures the good and the bad in almost equal measure. After all, maybe next time will be our time…

This series of books is a detailed and comprehensive history of the globe's most loved tournament. From its earliest beginnings and inauguration in the cold Uruguayan winter back in 1930 to its latest incarnation in Brazil 2014, no tournament is left uncovered. Here is every goal ever scored, both in qualifying and in the finals themselves, every controversy, every ugly confrontation, every glorious triumph, every iconic moment, every piece of unforgettable football genius. Any question you could possibly have about the World Cup is answered here. Also included in the final book of the series are some all-time team selections for all the major contenders throughout its history – no facts there, just good old opinion, whether you agree with it or not! The best players, goals and starting XI s at the end of each World Cup tournament are also my own selections, rather than the often dubious ones picked by FIFA (Oliver Kahn over Ronaldo in 2002 anyone?). But that, of course, is just another reason why the World Cup is so great: for footie fans young and old it is an endless and much-loved talking point and the subject of constant debate. At least with this book you have all the facts and stats you need to hold your own in the unforgiving world that is World Cup chitchat! For decades to come the World Cup will continue to entice, delight, frustrate and elate in equal measure. I hope you, like me, will always treasure every moment.

1970: Mexico

Qualification

71 Entrants.
England qualified as holders.
Mexico qualified as hosts.

Europe

> ### Stat Attack
>
> For the first time, at least five confederations were guaranteed a place in the finals.

Group 1

Switzerland 1-0 Greece, Portugal 3-0 Romania, Romania 2-0 Switzerland, Greece 4-2 Portugal, Portugal 0-2 Switzerland, Greece 2-2 Romania, Portugal 2-2 Greece, Switzerland 0-1 Romania, Romania 1-0 Portugal, Greece 4-1 Switzerland, Switzerland 1-1 Portugal, Romania 1-1 Greece

	Pld	W	D	L	GF	GA	Pts
Romania	6	3	2	1	7	6	8
Greece	6	2	3	1	13	9	7
Switzerland	6	2	1	3	5	8	5
Portugal	6	1	2	3	8	10	4

Romania qualified.

Group 2

Denmark 0-3 Czechoslovakia, Czechoslovakia 1-0 Denmark, Republic of Ireland 1-2 Czechoslovakia, Hungary 2-0 Czechoslovakia, Denmark 2-0 Republic of Ireland, Republic of Ireland 1-2 Hungary, Denmark 3-2 Hungary, Czechoslovakia 3-3 Hungary, Czechoslovakia 3-0 Republic of Ireland, Republic of Ireland 1-1 Denmark, Hungary 3-0 Denmark, Hungary 4-0 Republic of Ireland

	Pld	W	D	L	GF	GA	Pts
Hungary	6	4	1	1	16	7	9
Czechoslovakia	6	4	1	1	12	6	9
Denmark	6	2	1	3	6	10	5
Republic of Ireland	6	0	1	5	3	14	1

Play-off (in France): Czechoslovakia 4-1 Hungary

Czechoslovakia qualified.

Group 3

Wales 0-1 Italy, East Germany 2-2 Italy, East Germany 2-1 Wales, Wales 1-3 East Germany, Italy 4-1 Wales, Italy 3-0 East Germany

	Pld	W	D	L	GF	GA	Pts
Italy	4	3	1	0	10	3	7
East Germany	4	2	1	1	7	7	5
Wales	4	0	0	4	3	10	0

Italy qualified.

Group 4

Northern Ireland 4-1 Turkey, Turkey 0-3 Northern Ireland, Northern Ireland 0-0 USSR, USSR 3-0 Turkey, USSR 2-0 Northern Ireland, Turkey 1-3 USSR

	Pld	W	D	L	GF	GA	Pts
USSR	4	3	1	0	8	1	7
Northern Ireland	4	2	1	1	7	3	5
Turkey	4	0	0	4	2	13	0

USSR qualified.

Group 5

Sweden 5-0 Norway, France 0-1 Norway, Norway 2-5 Sweden, Norway 1-3 France, Sweden 2-0 France, France 3-0 Sweden

	Pld	W	D	L	GF	GA	Pts
Sweden	4	3	0	1	12	5	6
France	4	2	0	2	6	4	4
Norway	4	1	0	3	4	13	2

Sweden qualified.

Group 6

Finland 1-2 Belgium, Yugoslavia 9-1 Finland, Belgium 6-1 Finland, Belgium 3-0 Yugoslavia, Yugoslavia 0-0 Spain, Spain 1-1 Belgium, Belgium 2-1 Spain, Spain 2-1 Yugoslavia, Finland 1-5 Yugoslavia, Finland 2-0 Spain, Spain 6-0 Finland, Yugoslavia 4-0 Belgium

	Pld	W	D	L	GF	GA	Pts
Belgium	6	4	1	1	14	8	9
Yugoslavia	6	3	1	2	19	7	7
Spain	6	2	2	2	10	6	6
Finland	6	1	0	5	6	28	2

Belgium qualified.

Group 7

Austria 7-1 Cyprus, Austria 0-2 West Germany, Scotland 2-1 Austria, Cyprus 0-1 West Germany, Cyprus 0-5 Scotland, Scotland 1-1 West Germany, Cyprus 1-2 Austria, West Germany 1-0 Austria, Scotland 8-0 Cyprus, West Germany 12-0 Cyprus, West Germany 3-2 Scotland, Austria 2-0 Scotland

	Pld	W	D	L	GF	GA	Pts
West Germany	6	5	1	0	20	3	11
Scotland	6	3	1	2	18	7	7
Austria	6	3	0	3	12	7	6
Cyprus	6	0	0	6	2	35	0

West Germany qualified.

Group 8

Luxembourg 0-2 Holland (in Holland), Bulgaria 2-0 Holland, Holland 4-0 Luxembourg, Poland 8-1 Luxembourg, Bulgaria 2-1 Luxembourg, Holland 1-0 Poland, Bulgaria 4-1 Poland, Poland 2-1 Holland, Luxembourg 1-5 Poland, Holland 1-1 Bulgaria, Poland 3-0 Bulgaria, Luxembourg 1-3 Bulgaria

	Pld	W	D	L	GF	GA	Pts
Bulgaria	6	4	1	1	12	7	9
Poland	6	4	0	2	19	8	8
Holland	6	3	1	2	9	5	7
Luxembourg	6	0	0	6	4	24	0

Bulgaria qualified.

South America

Group 1

Bolivia 3-1 Argentina, Peru 1-0 Argentina, Bolivia 2-1 Peru, Peru 3-0 Bolivia, Argentina 1-0 Bolivia, Argentina 2-2 Peru

11

	Pld	W	D	L	GF	GA	Pts
Peru	4	2	1	1	7	4	5
Bolivia	4	2	0	2	5	6	4
Argentina	4	1	1	2	4	6	3

Peru qualified.

Group 2

Colombia 3-0 Venezuela, Venezuela 1-1 Colombia, Venezuela 0-2 Paraguay, Colombia 0-2 Brazil, Venezuela 0-5 Brazil, Colombia 0-1 Paraguay, Paraguay 0-3 Brazil, Brazil 6-2 Colombia, Paraguay 1-0 Venezuela, Paraguay 2-1 Colombia, Brazil 6-0 Venezuela, Brazil 1-0 Paraguay

	Pld	W	D	L	GF	GA	Pts
Brazil	6	6	0	0	23	2	12
Paraguay	6	4	0	2	6	5	8
Colombia	6	1	1	4	7	12	3
Venezuela	6	0	1	5	1	18	1

Brazil qualified.

Group 3

Ecuador 0-2 Uruguay, Chile 0-0 Uruguay, Uruguay 1-0 Ecuador, Chile 4-1 Ecuador, Ecuador 1-1 Chile, Uruguay 2-0 Chile

	Pld	W	D	L	GF	GA	Pts
Uruguay	4	3	1	0	5	0	7
Chile	4	1	2	1	5	4	4
Ecuador	4	0	1	3	2	8	1

Uruguay qualified.

North and Central America

First Round

Group 1

Canada 4-0 Bermuda, Canada 4-2 USA, Bermuda 0-0 Canada, USA 1-0 Canada, USA 6-2 Bermuda, Bermuda 0-2 USA

	Pld	W	D	L	GF	GA	Pts
USA	4	3	0	1	11	6	6
Canada	4	2	1	1	8	3	5
Bermuda	4	0	1	3	2	12	1

USA qualified for second round.

Group 2

Guatemala 4-0 Trinidad and Tobago, Trinidad and Tobago 0-0 Guatemala (in Guatemala), Trinidad and Tobago 0-4 Haiti (in Haiti), Haiti 2-4 Trinidad and Tobago, Haiti 2-0 Guatemala, Guatemala 1-1 Haiti

	Pld	W	D	L	GF	GA	Pts
Haiti	4	2	1	1	9	5	5
Guatemala	4	1	2	1	5	3	4
Trinidad and Tobago	4	1	1	2	4	10	3

Haiti qualified for second round.

Group 3

Costa Rica 3-0 Jamaica, Jamaica 1-3 Costa Rica (in Costa Rica), Honduras 3-1 Jamaica, Jamaica 0-2 Honduras (in Honduras), Honduras 1-0 Costa Rica, Costa Rica 1-1 Honduras

	Pld	W	D	L	GF	GA	Pts
Honduras	4	3	1	0	7	2	7
Costa Rica	4	2	1	1	7	3	5
Jamaica	4	0	0	4	2	11	0

Honduras qualified for second round.

Group 4

Dutch Guiana 6-0 Dutch Antilles, El Salvador 6-0 Dutch Guiana, Dutch Antilles 2-0 Dutch Guiana, El Salvador 1-0 Dutch Antilles, Dutch Antilles 1-2 El Salvador (in El Salvador), Dutch Guiana 4-1 El Salvador

	Pld	W	D	L	GF	GA	Pts
El Salvador	4	3	0	1	10	5	6
Dutch Guiana	4	2	0	2	10	9	4
Dutch Antilles	4	1	0	3	3	9	2

El Salvador qualified for second round.

Second Round

Group 1

Haiti 2-0 USA, USA 0-1 Haiti

	Pld	W	D	L	GF	GA	Pts
Haiti	2	2	0	0	3	0	4
USA	2	0	0	2	0	3	0

Haiti qualified for final round.

Group 2

Honduras 1-0 El Salvador, El Salvador 3-0 Honduras

	Pld	W	D	L	GF	GA	Pts
El Salvador	2	1	0	1	3	1	2
Honduras	2	1	0	1	1	3	2

Play-off (in Mexico): El Salvador 3-2 Honduras (aet)

El Salvador qualified for final round.

Only at the World Cup

The matches between El Salvador and Honduras were played in such a bad spirit that they aggravated tensions between the two countries to such an extent that a bitter four-day war was fought between the two known as the "Football War", which saw more than 2,000 people killed, most of them civilians. Still think England v Argentina is bad-tempered then?

Final Round

Haiti 1-2 El Salvador, El Salvador 0-3 Haiti

	Pld	W	D	L	GF	GA	Pts
Haiti	2	1	0	1	4	2	2
El Salvador	2	1	0	1	2	4	2

Play-off (in Jamaica): El Salvador 1-0 Haiti (aet)

El Salvador qualified.

Africa

First Round

Ghana received bye.
Zambia v Sudan: 4-2, 2-4 (aet) (agg. 6-6, Sudan won by more goals in second match)
Algeria v Tunisia: 1-2, 0-0 (agg. 1-2)
Nigeria v Cameroon: 1-1, 3-2 (agg. 4-3)
Libya v Ethiopia: 2-0, 1-5 (agg. 3-5)
Morocco v Senegal: 1-0, 1-2 (agg. 2-2) Play-off (in Canaries): Morocco 2-0 Senegal

Ghana, Sudan, Tunisia, Nigeria, Ethiopia and Morocco qualified for second round.

Second Round

Ethiopia v Sudan: 1-1, 1-3 (agg. 2-4)
Nigeria v Ghana: 2-1, 1-1 (agg. 3-2)
Tunisia v Morocco: 0-0, 0-0 (aet) (agg. 0-0) Play-off (in France): Morocco 2-2 Tunisia (aet) (Morocco won on toss of coin)

Sudan, Nigeria and Morocco qualified for final round.

Final Round

Nigeria 2-2 Sudan, Morocco 2-1 Nigeria, Sudan 3-3 Nigeria, Sudan 0-0 Morocco, Morocco 3-0 Sudan, Nigeria 2-0 Morocco

	Pld	W	D	L	GF	GA	Pts
Morocco	4	2	1	1	5	3	5
Nigeria	4	1	2	1	8	7	4
Sudan	4	0	3	1	5	8	3

Morocco qualified.

Asia and Oceania

First Round (in South Korea)

North Korea refused to play Israel and withdrew.
Israel, New Zealand and Rhodesia received byes.

Australia 3-1 Japan, South Korea 2-2 Japan, South Korea 1-2 Australia, Japan 1-1 Australia, South Korea 2-0 Japan, South Korea 1-1 Australia

	Pld	W	D	L	GF	GA	Pts
Australia	4	2	2	0	7	4	6
South Korea	4	1	2	1	6	5	4
Japan	4	0	2	2	4	8	2

Australia qualified for second round.

Second Round

Australia v Rhodesia (in Mozambique): 1-1, 0-0 (agg. 1-1) Play-off (in Mozambique): Australia 3-1 Rhodesia
Israel v New Zealand (in Israel): 4-0, 2-0 (agg. 6-0)

Australia and Israel qualified for final round.

Final Round

Israel v Australia: 1-0, 1-1 (agg. 2-1)

Israel qualified.

The Contenders

Belgium	Mexico
Brazil	Morocco
Bulgaria	Peru
Czechoslovakia	Romania
El Salvador	Sweden
England	Uruguay
Israel	USSR
Italy	West Germany

For the first time ever, the World Cup left its traditional host continents of Europe and South America and headed to Mexico in Central America. An ever-growing worldwide television audience meant that matches were scheduled for the middle of the day, meaning the intense heat would join the altitude as major issues for the competing teams, particularly the Europeans, for whom such conditions would be completely alien. Mexico 1970 would also mark the first time the World Cup was a truly global event thanks to FIFA's commendable decision to ensure that at least five of the continental confederations would be represented in the tournament.

The format of the competition remained identical to that established in the previous two tournaments. However, the draw had been unseeded, resulting in some very uneven groups. There would be some better innovations showcased, however. For the first time, matches would be broadcast in colour (although colour footage of much of the 1966 tournament does exist) while substitutes and yellow and red cards would also make their World Cup debut. Mexico, meanwhile, had just hosted a highly successful Olympic Games in 1968 and the experience gained would no doubt prove beneficial to the World Cup. Everything looked in place for an exciting tournament.

Hosts **Mexico**, drawn in Group One, would enjoy the advantage of playing their games at Mexico City's gigantic Azteca stadium, which would be able to cram in more than 105,000 of their passionate fans. Still, with a dismal tournament record, they would certainly have a job on their hands keeping up the tradition that every host nation always made it through the first round. Home advantage would no doubt help but their squad looked little better than those which had struggled repeatedly in previous World Cups. At least in goalkeeper Ignacio Calderon, defender Gustavo Pena and striker Enrique Borja they had players with World Cup experience and who had done their reputations no harm with their performances in England 1966. The weakness of their group would also help but still, reaching the quarter-finals would be a tough assignment.

Stat Attack

For the first time in a World Cup, substitutions were allowed. The use of yellow and red cards to signify bookings and sendings off was also new. These had been invented by English referee Ken Aston after the confusion of the England-Argentina game in 1966.

Group favourites undoubtedly were the **USSR**, who had never failed to reach the quarter-finals of the World Cup. Veteran goalkeeper Lev Yashin was still in the squad and, though unlikely to play, his winning mentality and presence would surely be a positive factor on the squad, in particular on the man most likely to take the starting spot between the sticks, Anzor Kavazashvili. Kavazashvili would be protected by a formidable defence, including fellow Georgians Murtaz Khurtsilava and Revaz Dzodzuashvili, as well as the dominant Albert Shesternev. The Soviets would also pack a punch further forward with potent Ukrainian Anatoliy Byshovets looking the pick of their attacking options. Again, a serious challenge looked likely.

Belgium would also fancy their chances of progressing from the group. Qualifying for their first finals in 16 years courtesy of beating both Yugoslavia and Spain, they were a highly capable team. In Paul Van Himst they had an incredibly potent attacking weapon while Wilfried Van Moer was developing into a fine midfielder. They could well be a match for the Soviets.

The fourth side in the group, **El Salvador**, looked like guaranteed whipping boys and easy pickings for the other three sides. First-time qualifiers, no doubt helped by Mexico's absence from the Central American qualifying zone, their progress ahead of neighbours Honduras had actually sparked a short and bloody war which had claimed the lives of nearly a thousand of the country's civilians. They would be eager to do their beleaguered people justice, though they had already far exceeded expectations simply by reaching the finals. If they could make further progress, it would be a massive shock.

Group Two would take place in the high-altitude venues of Toluca and Puebla and would most likely not see breathtaking footballing, with the group's two favourites both renowned for their attention to all-out defence. The more fancied of these two were European champions **Italy**, who at least had quality to back up their frequently negative and occasionally brutal tactics. Foremost amongst them were playmakers Gianni Rivera and Sandro Mazzola, although coach Ferruccio Valcareggi believed the two could not play together, despite having done so successfully before, and vowed he would only play one at a time. Still, whichever one started would be a major creative weapon for the Azzurri and in deadly Cagliari winger or striker Luigi Riva he would also have a top-class goalscorer. Naturally, the Italians were also rock solid at the back, with exceptional Inter full backs Tarcisio Burgnich and Giacinto Facchetti to the fore, while defensive midfielder

Mario Bertini was acquiring a reputation as a brutal and uncompromising opponent who would let no-one past him. Everything looked in place for a long-overdue run in the tournament: Italy had failed to get past the first round since 1938, the last time they won the competition.

Their biggest challengers in the group would be **Uruguay**, who also were famous for their tough defence and brutal tactics. With star keeper Ladislao Mazurkiewicz protected by a formidable quartet of Luis Ubinas, Atilio Ancheta, Roberto Matosas and Juan Mujica, they would be incredibly tough to score against. Further forward, brilliant playmaker Pedro Rocha would be travelling to his third World Cup despite being only 27, while in darting winger Luis Cubilla he had an able attacking accomplice. They looked a well-balanced and capable side and would be tough to beat.

Returning to the World Cup for the first time since finishing runners-up on home soil in 1958, **Sweden** would be coached by one of the heroes of that side, right-back Orvar Bergmark. The Scandinavians certainly did not have a squad of that level of ability but nevertheless, they could call upon several talented players, including playmaker Bo Larsson, striker Ove Kindvall and centre-back Bjorn Nordqvist. They would enter the tournament with at least some hope of reaching the quarter-finals.

Intriguingly, **Israel** would be the fourth side in the group. They would at least come with experience, having surprised everyone by reaching the quarter-finals of the 1968 Olympics in Mexico City, but there looked little chance of them beating any of the other three sides in their group, even with the goal threat of striker Mordechai Spiegler. Still, they would be out to enjoy their World Cup debut.

By far the most competitive of the groups would surely be Group Three in Guadalajara, which featured holders England, favourites Brazil and solid teams Czechoslovakia and Romania, who had accounted for Olympic champions Hungary and Eusebio's Portugal respectively in qualifying. **England** seemed to have a fantastic chance of defending their trophy. Widely considered a better side than in 1966, their key players from the triumph on home soil, Gordon Banks, Bobby Moore, Bobby Charlton, Geoff Hurst, Alan Ball and Martin Peters, would all still be central to Alf Ramsey's plans. The coach could also call upon a pair of phenomenal attacking full-backs in Keith Newton and Terry Cooper, a hugely-talented midfield enforcer in Alan Mullery and a prolific goal scorer in Francis Lee. With World Cup winners Nobby Stiles and Jack Charlton likely only to bc warming the bench, England had both great depth and immense talent. They were the team to beat.

England would face formidable opponents in **Brazil**. With Mario Zagallo installed as coach, they would be able to call upon Pelé, who Zagallo had successfully persuaded to travel to the tournament, and the world's best player, now 29, would be able to demonstrate the full range of his talents. He would not lack support either. Assisting the great man would be an array of world-class playmakers and forwards, among them the intelligent Tostao, the visionary Gerson and the quick-footed Jairzinho, all given cameos in 1966, and new midfield star Roberto Rivelino, a fabulously gifted playmaker who could also be deployed wide on the left, as looked likely in order to also accommodate Gerson. With such a huge level of talent in their side, it was no surprise Zagallo's team were hot favourites for the title.

Czechoslovakia also looked a very capable side, still bossed by veteran playmaker Andrej Kvasnak. With Ladislav Petras and Jozef Adamec,

> ## Only at the World Cup
>
> England's World Cup preparations were disrupted when Bobby Moore was accused of stealing a bracelet when the squad were out preparing in Colombia. Moore spent several days under house arrest before he was eventually released on bail and allowed to rejoin the squad. The charges against him, which were largely believed to be unfounded, were later dropped.

they would score goals, while keeper Ivo Viktor and star defender Karol Dobias would take no prisoners at the other end. They looked strong across the park but the bad luck of the draw meant they would have to beat Brazil or England if they were to reach the next round and this was improbable.

The fourth member of the group, **Romania**, would also come with genuine hopes of progressing with a fine side in their own right. Florea Dumitrache and Mircea Lucescu looked set to bag a few goals, even against tough opponents, while the presence of solid centre-back Cornel Dinu would keep them tight at the other end. Nevertheless, it seemed unlikely they would be able to edge out either of the two heavyweights of world football in their group to claim a quarter-final place.

At Leon, **West Germany** were overwhelming favourites to clean up in Group Four. Helmut Schon's side looked greatly improved from the already fine outfit who had finished runners-up in 1966 and had been devastating in qualifying. Veteran Uwe Seeler would play at his fourth World Cup and he would be assisted in the goalscoring department by the squat but prolific Bayern Munich star Gerd Muller. Franz Beckenbauer, now an established star, and Wolfgang Overath would play in a phenomenal midfield, while the likes of Karl-Heinz Schnellinger, Willi Schulz and the tenacious Berti Vogts would form a solid barrier in front of star keeper Sepp Maier. They looked like being one of the favourites to win the competition.

Facing them would be **Peru**, who had reached their first World Cup since the inaugural competition in 1930. Managed by Brazilian legend Didi, they had accounted for Argentina in qualifying and were gaining a reputation as a side focused on all-out and skilled attack. With their gung-ho attitude and talented players, they would be a thrilling team to watch. Spearheading their challenge was hugely gifted 21-year-old attacking midfielder or occasional striker Teofilo Cubillas and the dangerous Alberto Gallardo, while Hector Chumpitaz would look to keep things secure at the back. Their exciting young side could be dark horses to make a real impact at the competition.

Bulgaria had made it to their third successive World Cup and would come hoping to lose their reputation as a negative and cynical side. They had qualified impressively ahead of highly capable Poland and Holland teams and in Georgi Asparoukhov they had a massively talented striker. With Dimitar Yakimov his supplier and Aleksandar Shalamanov and Boris Gaganelov shoring things up at the back, this time there looked genuine cause for Bulgarian optimism.

Africa's representation was provided by **Morocco**, the first side to benefit from FIFA's decision to give the continent a guaranteed place in the finals in the wake of the mass boycott of African teams from the 1966 competition. The Moroccans had been somewhat fortunate to make it this far, only scraping past Tunisia on the toss of a coin, but now that they were here they were determined to do their continent proud. An unknown quantity, they would do their best to ruffle a few feathers on their World Cup debut.

> ### Stat Attack
>
> Morocco were the first African side to reach the finals since Egypt in 1934.

Debutants: El Salvador, Israel, Morocco

The Draw

Group 1
Belgium
El Salvador
Mexico
USSR

Group 2
Israel
Italy
Sweden
Uruguay

Group 3
Brazil
Czechoslovakia
England
Romania

Group 4
Bulgaria
Morocco
Peru
West Germany

Venues:
Mexico City, Guadalajara, Leon, Puebla, Toluca

The Tournament – 31 May-21 June

Group Stage – First series

Hosts **Mexico** got the tournament kick-started against the **USSR**, on paper the strongest of their group opponents. Playing them first was probably an advantage for the Mexicans, as the Soviets were understandably cautious as they looked to play themselves into form and get used to the alien conditions. It was hardly surprising, then, that the home side had the better of the first half, Horacio Lopez having the best chance but directing his close-range header straight at Anzor Kavazashvili. However, it was the Soviets who were much the better team in the second 45 minutes. Acclimatising to the heat, Anatoliy Byshovets had an effort well tipped away by Ignacio Calderon before wasting the best chance of the match when sending a free header wide late on. 0-0 was probably a fair reflection of the game and probably a good result for the hosts against their strongest opponents but those in attendance were greatly disappointed by the lifeless spectacle.

> ### Stat Attack
>
> This match featured the first substitution in World Cup history, Anatoliy Puzach brought on for Viktor Serebryanikov at half-time.

Up in the heights of Puebla, **Uruguay** started surprisingly brightly against **Israel**, showing uncharacteristic attacking ambition, with full-backs Luis Ubinas and Juan Mujica raiding down the flanks to great effect. However, the South Americans suffered an early blow when their captain and

20

star playmaker Pedro Rocha had to be stretchered off with a serious injury barely 10 minutes in and he would likely miss the rest of the tournament. Nevertheless, Uruguay did not let this affect them and took a deserved lead midway through the half. Roberto Matosas' pass was knocked into the path of Mujica by midfielder Julio Montero Castillo and Ubinas' run to the far post distracted the Israeli defence, giving Ildo Maneiro the chance to convert the cross. In the second half, Ubinas and Mujica teamed up to create a second goal. Ubinas' deep cross reached Maneiro and though Yitzchak Vissoker parried his shot, Mujica burst in to smash home the rebound. Uruguay had won impressively and served notice they would be a threat in the tournament. However, losing Rocha was a big blow.

Holders **England** started their tournament against a capable **Romania** side. Having at last put the Bobby Moore theft saga to bed, they won comfortably. Fielding their first-choice starting line-up, they outclassed their dogged opponents all over the pitch but it wasn't until well into the second half that they finally broke the deadlock, Geoff Hurst popping up with the goal to seal victory. They could have scored more but England were clearly saving themselves for tougher assignments ahead.

In Leon, **Peru** provided instant sensation, playing beautifully uninhibited football and fighting back from two goals down to improbably beat a fine **Bulgaria** team. Peru's capital Lima had been devastated by a major earthquake days earlier and the tragedy, fresh in the minds of the players, may well have contributed to their sluggish start. Bulgaria took full advantage, taking an early lead with a superb free-kick routine. Dimitar Yakimov rolled the ball to the lurking Hristo Bonev and his sublime flicked back-heel released Dinko Dermendzhiev to fire past Luis Rubinos for 1-0. Four minutes into the second half and Peru's predicament became desperate when Bulgaria won another free-kick on the edge of the area and Bonev fired it past the hesitant Rubinos. However, Peru's dynamite attack struck a crucial blow just a minute later, left winger Alberto Gallardo rifling his shot powerfully into the top corner from wide out. Five minutes later, Didi's side had conjured an improbable equaliser. When Hugo Sotil was tripped on the edge of the area, centre-back Hector Chumpitaz stepped up and poked the ball into the corner from the free-kick. Bulgaria were reeling and Peru's answer to Pelé, Teofilo Cubillas, dealt the final blow with 15 minutes left, dribbling past two men and smashing past the stunned Simeon Simeonov for a 3-2 victory. Bulgaria's hopes of a first World Cup win had been dashed but the crowd had been captivated by Peru's attacking freedom and skill.

Back in Mexico City's Azteca stadium, little **El Salvador** made their World Cup debut against **Belgium**. They struggled manfully but were eventually overwhelmed by the Europeans' mixture of grit and skill. Wilfried Van Moer scored early on from fully 35 yards, though in truth keeper Raul Magana should have done better. Magana briefly redeemed himself when brilliantly tipping over another Van Moer piledriver in the second half but a horrible error from the keeper did gift the midfielder a second goal soon after, completely missing Leon Semmeling's cross and Van Moer tapping into the empty net. Belgium's star man Paul Van Himst twice missed fantastic chances to increase the lead before El Salvador almost pulled one back through Ernesto Aparicio but keeper Christian Piot was quickly out to deny the striker. Instead, Belgium got a fortunate third, Semmeling winning a dubious penalty which Raoul Lambert smashed into the corner. They had won comfortably but had not been particularly impressive.

High up in Toluca, **Italy** and **Sweden** played out a desperately poor Group Two encounter. All the action of note took place in the first ten minutes, when Luigi Riva hit the post before young Sweden keeper Ronnie Hellstrom somehow let Angelo Domenghini's weak shot from range squirm through his grasp into the back of the net. Sweden did get the ball into the net in the second half but the effort was chalked off for offside. Both sides tired in the rarefied air, however, and most of the game was played at a walking pace with virtually no excitement.

Brazil swaggered into Guadalajara and quickly showed exactly why they were tournament favourites, demolishing a very fine **Czechoslovakia** side 4-1. However, they started poorly and striker Ladislav Petras put the Europeans ahead early on, bursting past centre back Brito and smashing high past Felix into the roof of the net. Nevertheless, Brazil came storming back. Pele was fouled on the edge of the area and Roberto Rivelino stepped up to hammer a thunderbolt left-foot shot past the helpless Ivo Viktor. The Brazilians were gradually clicking into exhibition mode and Pelé almost put his side ahead with an audacious lob from his own half which drifted just wide. In the second half, Brazil went for the throat, Pelé beautifully teeing up midfielder Gerson, whose power-drive left Viktor hopelessly beaten but came back off the post. The Czechs were hanging on but Gerson's visionary passing was to finish them. One incredible ball over the top was beautifully controlled on his chest by Pelé before the great man smashed it in gloriously on the half-volley. Gerson was at it again just two minutes later, his long, looping pass catching out everyone and Jairzinho flicking the ball over Viktor and firing it in. With a goal to his name, Jairzinho became all but unstoppable and soon scored a sublime second. Picking the ball up on the halfway line, the winger dribbled effortlessly through three defenders before slotting the ball into the far corner. Anyone wondering what Brazil's 1970 vintage were capable of had been shown their quality in no uncertain terms.

Back in Leon, **West Germany** were desperately lucky to come away with victory over a **Morocco** side they had clearly underestimated. The Germans probed cautiously for 20 minutes without finding an opening before the Africans stole the ball off them, broke quickly upfield and put in a dangerous cross which Horst-Dieter Hottges horrendously headed back across goal, allowing Mohammed Houmane the simplest of tap-ins to give the North Africans a shock lead. Suddenly the game opened up and both teams could have scored before half-time, Germany's Gerd Muller uncharacteristically wasting some good openings. In the second period, the Europeans finally broke the stubborn Africans' resistance. Siggi Held found Muller in the area and the striker coolly found Uwe Seeler to fire home an equaliser. Germany kept pushing forward and were rewarded with the winner when Jurgen Grabowski's deep cross was headed against the bar by Held but the predatory Muller was there like the true goal poacher he was to head in the rebound from a yard out. West Germany had their opening victory but the Moroccans could be incredibly proud of their efforts.

Group Stage – Second series

At the Azteca, a crunch match ensued between two European sides, the **USSR** and **Belgium**. The Belgians had the chance to take a crucial early lead but the usually reliable Wilfried Van Moer produced a shocking double miss. Anatoliy Byshovets soon punished his wasteful finishing by powerfully beating Christian Piot to put the Soviets ahead. In the second half, it was the Soviet Union who ran away with it with three goals of the highest quality. First, Georgian midfielder Kakhi Asatiani stepped his way past Georges Heylens wide on the left and struck a fabulous shot into the far corner. Byshovets then eclipsed

even this with a wonder strike, cutting in from the right and cracking in an unstoppable effort past the helpless Piot. The massacre was complete when striker Vitaly Khmelnitsky played a quick one-two to the right and met the return pass with a fine stooping header into the far corner. The 4-0 scoreline was incredibly tough on Belgium, who certainly played their part, and at least they did manage a late consolation, Van Moer's swerving effort from 30 yards coming back off the post and Raoul Lambert tapping in the rebound. However, they had been well beaten while the Soviets had secured a place in the quarter-finals.

In Group Two, **Italy** and **Uruguay** inevitably played out the 0-0 draw everyone expected. International football's two defensive masters were never likely to commit many players to attack and certainly not enough to breach each other's formidable defences. A desperately dull game did thankfully pass without the violence sometimes associated with the teams but also without almost any excitement. The fans at Puebla surely lost interest long before the end.

In the intense heat of Guadalajara, Europeans **Czechoslovakia** and **Romania** struggled. Both desperately needed a victory to keep their hopes of reaching the quarter-finals alive but the conditions were not conducive to the hard-running football both liked to play. Still, the Czechs took an early lead when Ladislav Petras headed them in front after five minutes. Largely the better side, they clung on until five minutes into the second period, when Alexandru Neagu finally got the ball in the net for the Romanians. Galvanised by their equaliser, they went in search of a winner and found it when Florea Dumitrache converted a penalty. They had won but the result was harsh on the Czechs, who had been undone by their lack of preparation time.

Group Four saw **Peru** book their place in the quarter-finals with a hard-fought victory over **Morocco**, who again proved themselves more than worthy of their place in the finals. For 65 minutes they had the South Americans on the back foot and were desperately unfortunate to go behind when a lucky deflection off a post left Teofilo Cubillas with the simplest of close-range finishes. The North Africans continued to hassle Peru but their hopes were dashed two minutes later when midfielder Roberto Challe superbly danced his way through their defence before delicately lifting the ball over keeper Allal Kassou for a top-class goal. Peru added a third late on, Cubillas racing onto Hugo Sotil's lay-off to hammer past Kassou once more. They had won comfortably enough in the end but Morocco had more than played their part and were hugely unfortunate to lose by the three-goal margin.

In front of their passionate hordes in the Azteca, **Mexico** cruised to victory over fellow Central Americans **El Salvador**, albeit in controversial fashion. The little Salvadorans resisted the hosts' attacks for 45 minutes and seconds before half-time were awarded a free-kick deep in their own half. However, Mexico's Aaron Padilla quickly took the kick, crossing for Javier Valdivia to fire home at the far post. Incredibly, Egyptian referee Ali Kandil allowed the goal to stand, despite the Salvadorans' furious protest. Their players thumped the resulting kick-off into the crowd as a show of their fury at the decision and promptly collapsed in the second half.

> ## Only at the World Cup
>
> This match was to see one of the most scandalous decisions of any World Cup, Egyptian referee Kandil the guilty man. He awarded El Salvador a free-kick in their own half but Mexican forward Padilla took it instead and passed for Valdivia to score. However, the referee did not disallow the clearly illegal goal, refusing El Salvador's protests. Understandably, the furious Salvadorans fell apart after this.

> ## Stat Attack
>
> Juan Ignacio Basaguren became the first substitute to score in the World Cup.

Valdivia notched his second in impressive fashion in the first minute of the second period and Javier Fragoso had soon made it three, tucking in Horacio Lopez's knockdown. It was 4-0 by the end, substitute Juan Ignacio Basaguren converting Valdivia's pass from close in. However, the performance of referee Kandil had been questionable to say the least.

Toluca saw **Sweden** and **Israel** search for the victory both needed to realistically keep alive their hopes of reaching the next stage. The match was an intensely physical affair, with the Israelis disgracefully hacking down their opponents at almost every opportunity, though the Scandinavians were not totally blameless themselves. The worst incident saw striker Mordechai Spiegler, who had just gone on an impressive jinking run, savagely kick keeper Sven-Gunnar Larsson, receiving only a booking for the offence. Sweden had taken the lead minutes earlier when Tom Turesson tapped in right-back Hans Selander's cross but with Larsson's movement impeded by his injury, Spiegler himself equalised seconds after injuring the keeper, firing into the corner from the edge of the area. The Israelis held on for a point they probably deserved, though the manner in which they had played hardly built them a reputation as a good footballing side.

In Guadalajara, two of the greatest sides in the history of World Cup football played out an enthralling battle in one of the all-time great World Cup matches. World champions **England** faced **Brazil**, the team many tipped to succeed them as the tournament winners. The hot conditions were a handicap to England but nevertheless, they adapted fantastically, dropping their tempo to play a more South American-style passing game. The move worked perfectly and they dominated the match but struggled

> ## Only at the World Cup
>
> Gordon Banks produced the "save of the century" to deny Pelé. The striker was clearly shouting "Goal!" as he sent a bullet header at goal but Banks threw himself down and backwards to just flick the ball over the bar with his thumb. Pelé later said that it was the greatest save he had ever seen.

to take the lead. Francis Lee twice came agonisingly close in the first half but the best opportunity came at the other end. Jairzinho skinned Terry Cooper on the right wing and crossed for Pelé to bullet a header at goal, only for Gordon Banks to somehow throw himself down and tip the ball over the bar for a fantastic save. In the second half, the probing Brazilians took the lead, finally breaching the resolute England defence. Tostao dribbled into the area and his pass picked out Pelé. The great number ten spotted Jairzinho to his right and cleverly drew his man before sliding the ball to the winger to fire past the Herculean Banks. All was not yet lost for England, however. Still the better side, Bobby Moore produced the tackle of the tournament to dispossess the tricky Jairzinho with perfect timing before starting a move which saw substitute striker Jeff Astle freed in the box but the West Brom man somehow shooting wide of a virtually open goal. Another Moore pass picked out

> ## Only at the World Cup
>
> Pelé and Bobby Moore produced what is probably the most famous World Cup image ever when the two greats, beaming from ear to ear, embraced and swapped shirts at the end of the game, a symbol of the huge respect each had for the other.

Alan Ball in the area and his shot beat Felix but not the crossbar. England, despite dominating much of the game, had lost. They had been hugely unlucky but had played their part in an outstanding contest between two great teams. At the end, Pelé and Moore exchanged shirts, a sign of the appreciation each had for the other's skill. It was a truly wonderful moment.

West Germany matched Peru in reaching the quarter-finals after just two games, comfortably beating **Bulgaria**. They were given an early wake-up call, however, by another well-worked Bulgarian free-kick. Georgi Asparoukhov rolled the ball to the lurking Asparuh Nikodimov, who fired it past Sepp Maier to put the Eastern Europeans in front. However, Germany's right winger Reinhard Libuda was about to turn in an inspired performance to drag his team to victory. First, eight minutes after Germany had fallen behind, he ran to the by-line and pulled back across goal, an error from keeper Simeonov allowing the ball to cross the line before being hacked out by a defender. Clearly rattled by conceding such a goal, Bulgaria promptly let in another in almost identical fashion, Libuda again sliding the ball across the face and this time Gerd Muller arriving to tap in from a yard out. In the second half, Libuda continued to torment his opponents with his running. Once more he cut into the area and this time was brought down. Muller fired the spot-kick home for 3-1. Muller next turned provider, squaring for Uwe Seeler, who had been dropped back into midfield for the game, to slide home the Germans' fourth. The rout continued unabated when Libuda was again the provider, swinging in a free-kick from the right which Muller, totally unmarked, headed in to complete a hat-trick. The damage was done but a minute later Bulgaria did manage a late consolation, Todor Kolev smashing the ball into the roof of the net from the edge of the area. Nevertheless, Germany were winners by some distance and in the little hitman Muller they seemed to have a true penalty-box predator.

Group Stage – Third series

The **USSR** looked for a goal glut against **El Salvador** to set them up for the quarter-finals in the best possible fashion. Resting several players, however, they obviously did not consider it too tough a test. In the end they did win comfortably enough, 2-0, with both goals coming from the in-form Anatoliy Byshovets, but the Salvadorans matched them for large passages of the game and were anything but humiliated. They might not have been able to muster a point or a goal in the finals but they had avoided the hammering many had predicted.

In Group Two, **Sweden** knew that they had to beat **Uruguay** in Puebla to have any chance of reaching the next stage. They were forced to chase the game and commit men to attack but rather than attempting to hit the Scandinavians on the break, Uruguay played a depressingly negative game, pulling everybody back in an effort to keep the score at 0-0, with seemingly no ambition for anything other than the draw. Try as they might, Sweden couldn't break through such a tightly packed defence and promptly went out, although in the final seconds substitute Ove Grahn headed in Hans Selander's cross from close range. Sweden had won but it was a hollow victory. They finished with an inferior goal difference to Uruguay and were on the long flight home.

Guadalajara saw **Brazil** complete a clean-sweep of their group with victory over **Romania**. They took the lead when Pelé blasted home a powerful free-kick for his tenth World Cup goal and the South Americans' lead was doubled three minutes later when Paulo Cesar's mazy run on the left flank took him past the defender to the by-line and allowed him to cross for Jairzinho to convert. However, as brilliant as Brazil were going forward, they still had a tendency to go to sleep at the back, one such error allowing Florea Dumitrache to pounce and reduce the deficit to 2-1 at half-time. Brazil continued to attack with freedom and skill in the second period. From a corner, Tostao flicked the ball on and Pelé turned it home for 3-1. However, late on the Europeans again punished Brazil's defensive failings, Lajos Satmareanu crossing for Emerich Dembrovschi to head past the shaky Felix from close range. Brazil had won 3-2 but a better side than Romania might well have made them pay more dearly for their lack of concentration at the back.

Group Four saw **West Germany** and **Peru**, both already assured of qualification for the next stage, go head-to-head for top spot in the group. In a frantic first half, Uwe Seeler's spectacular bicycle kick from Reinhard Libuda's cross went just over the bar before another ball from Libuda was chested down by Gerd Muller and the Bayern Munich striker coolly beat the advancing Rubinos. Soon after, superb work down the left flank by Hannes Lohr saw the winger put in a cross that Muller swept home for 2-0. The stocky striker was soon celebrating a second successive hat-trick, meeting Seeler's cross with a powerful header, and Germany were in total control. However, Peru fought back late in the half. A strong run from defender Orlando de la Torre was halted on the edge of the box and Teofilo Cubillas' free-kick took an unfortunate deflection to creep past Sepp Maier. The second half, by contrast, was an uninspired affair, with both teams seemingly keen to preserve their energy for their quarter-finals and Peru unwilling to go all out in search of victory.

Back at the Azteca, **Mexico** just managed to scrape past **Belgium** to qualify for the quarter-finals, though again controversy reigned in Mexico City. 14 minutes in, Argentinean referee Coerezza awarded the hosts a highly dubious penalty which captain Gustavo Pena converted. The Belgians were furious but they could find no reply. Neither team could find another goal and so Mexico clung onto their deeply fortunate 1-0 lead all the way to the finish. They had reached the quarter-finals for the first time but they had clearly enjoyed some favours from referees along the way.

Toluca played host to another terribly dull Group Two clash, this time between **Italy** and **Israel**. The Italians, assured of progress unless they suffered heavy defeat, elected to defend in depth rather than seek to score themselves. Even the first appearance of the tournament for Gianni Rivera, surprisingly left out of the starting line-up for all three games but now finally brought on as a substitute, couldn't galvanise them. Israel, meanwhile, never looked like having the tools to worry the Italians and the game finished in yet another 0-0 draw. Clearly, Group Two had not been one for the football purists.

England booked their spot in the next stage with a gritty victory over **Czechoslovakia**. Playing in their unfamiliar light-blue third-choice strip, an England side showing several changes did enough to beat their fellow Europeans, though the match was anything but pretty. Eventually, it was one of the new arrivals, debutant striker Allan Clarke, who scored the only goal of the game from the penalty spot. The Czechs, on their way home, had no reply and the game petered out into something of a lifeless contest.

The last match of the group stages featured two sides who had already been eliminated, **Bulgaria** and **Morocco**. Understandably, neither played with much passion in another dull clash. The Bulgarians did take the lead with five minutes of the half remaining, again their free-kick routine serving them well. Vassil Mitkov rolled the ball to Dobromir Zhechev, who fired home. However, the brave Africans didn't give up and earned themselves a deserved second-half equaliser from the

boot of Maouhoub Ghazouani. They could be hugely proud of their performances at the World Cup and they had been unlucky not to do even better. Bulgaria, meanwhile, had shown signs of improvement but were still short of that elusive first World Cup win.

First Round results

Group 1

Mexico 0-0 USSR
31/05/70 – Mexico City (Azteca)
Mexico: Calderon, Vantolra, Pena (c), Guzman, Perez, Hernandez, Pulido, Velarde (Munguia), Valdivia, Fragoso, Lopez
USSR: Kavazashvili, Kaplichny, Logofet, Shesternev (c), Lovchev, Asatiani, Muntian, Serebryanikov (Puzach), Byshovets, Yevriuzhikin, Nodia (Khmelnitsky)
Referee: Tschenscher (West Germany)

Belgium 3-0 El Salvador
03/06/70 – Mexico City (Azteca)
Belgium: Piot, Heylens, Dewalque, Dockx, Thissen, Semmeling (Polleunis), Van Moer, Van Himst (c), Devrindt, Puis, Lambert
Goals: Van Moer 12, 54, Lambert pen 76
El Salvador: Magana, Rivas, Mariona (c), Osorio, Manzano (Cortes), Quintanilla, Vasquez, Martinez, Rodriguez (Sermeno), Cabezas, Aparicio
Referee: Radulescu (Romania)

USSR 4-1 Belgium
06/06/70 – Mexico City (Azteca)
USSR: Kavazashvili, Kaplichny (Lovchev), Dzodzuashvili (Kiselev), Shesternev (c), Afonin, Asatiani, Muntian, Khurtsilava, Byshovets, Yevriuzhikin, Khmelnitsky
Goals: Byshovets 14, 63, Asatiani 57, Khmelnitsky 76
Belgium: Piot, Heylens, Dewalque, Dockx, Thissen, Semmeling, Jeck, Van Moer, Van Himst (c), Puis, Lambert
Goals: Lambert 86
Referee: Scheurer (Switzerland)

Mexico 4-0 El Salvador
07/06/70 – Mexico City (Azteca)
Mexico: Calderon, Vantolra, Pena (c), Guzman, Perez, Gonzalez, Munguia, Valdivia, Borja (Lopez) (Basaguren), Fragoso, Padilla
Goals: Valdivia 45, 46, Fragoso 58, Basaguren 83
El Salvador: Magana, Rivas, Mariona (c), Osorio, Cortes (Monge), Quintanilla, Vasquez, Martinez, Rodriguez, Cabezas, Aparicio (Mendez)
Referee: Kandil (Egypt)

USSR 2-0 El Salvador
10/06/70 – Mexico City (Azteca)
USSR: Kavazashvili, Dzodzuashvili, Khurtsilava, Shesternev (c), Afonin, Kiselev (Asatiani), Muntian, Serebryanikov, Byshovets, Puzach (Yevriuzhikin), Khmelnitsky
Goals: Byshovets 51, 74
El Salvador: Magana, Rivas, Mariona (c), Osorio, Castro, Mendez, Vasquez, Portillo, Rodriguez (Sermeno), Cabezas (Aparicio), Monge
Referee: Hormazabal (Chile)

Mexico 1-0 Belgium

11/06/70 – Mexico City (Azteca)

Mexico: Calderon, Vantolra, Pena (c), Guzman, Perez, Gonzalez, Pulido, Munguia, Valdivia (Basaguren), Fragoso, Padilla

Goals: Pena pen 14

Belgium: Piot, Heylens, Dewalque, Dockx, Thissen, Semmeling, Jeck, Van Moer, Van Himst (c), Puis, Polleunis (Devrindt)

Referee: Coerezza (Argentina)

	Pld	W	D	L	GF	GA	Pts
USSR	3	2	1	0	6	1	5
Mexico	3	2	1	0	5	0	5
Belgium	3	1	0	2	4	5	2
El Salvador	3	0	0	3	0	9	0

USSR and Mexico qualified for quarter-finals.

Group 2

Stat Attack

As FIFA had not yet declared goals scored as a way of separating teams whose goal difference was identical, the USSR topped the group by the drawing of lots.

Uruguay 2-0 Israel

02/06/70 – Puebla (Cuauhtemoc)

Uruguay: Mazurkiewicz, Ubinas, Ancheta, Matosas, Mujica, Maneiro, Montero Castillo, Rocha (c) (Cortes), Cubilla, Esparrago, Losada

Goals: Maneiro 23, Mujica 50

Israel: Vissoker, Schwager, Rosen, Rosenthal, Primo, Shum, Spiegel (c), Talbi (Bar), Spiegler, Feigenbaum, Rom (Vollach)

Referee: Davidson (Scotland)

Italy 1-0 Sweden

03/06/70 – Toluca (La Bombonera)

Italy: Albertosi, Burgnich, Cera, Niccolai (Rosato), Facchetti (c), Bertini, Mazzola, De Sisti, Domenghini, Boninsegna, Riva

Goals: Domenghini 10

Sweden: Hellstrom, Olsson, Axelsson, Nordqvist (c), Grip, Svensson, B Larsson (Nicklasson), Eriksson (Ejderstedt), Kindvall, Grahn, Cronqvist

Referee: Taylor (England)

Uruguay 0-0 Italy

06/06/70 – Puebla (Cuauhtemoc)

Uruguay: Mazurkiewicz, Ubinas (c), Ancheta, Matosas, Mujica, Maneiro, Montero Castillo, Cortes, Cubilla, Esparrago, Bareno (Zubia)

Italy: Albertosi, Burgnich, Cera, Rosato, Facchetti (c), Bertini, Mazzola, De Sisti, Domenghini (Furino), Boninsegna, Riva

Referee: Glockner (East Germany)

Sweden 1-1 Israel
07/06/70 – Toluca (La Bombonera)
Sweden: S Larsson, Selander, Axelsson, Olsson, Grip, Svensson (c), B Larsson, Nordahl, Turesson, Kindvall, Persson (Palsson)
Goals: Turesson 53
Israel: Vissoker, Bar, Vollach (Shuruk), Rosen, Primo, Schwager, Rosenthal, Shum, Spiegel, Spiegler (c), Feigenbaum
Goals: Spiegler 56
Referee: Tarekegn (Ethiopia)

Sweden 1-0 Uruguay
10/06/70 – Puebla (Cuauhtemoc)
Sweden: S Larsson, Selander, Axelsson, Nordqvist (c), Grip, Svensson, B Larsson, Eriksson, Kindvall (Turesson), Nicklasson (Grahn), Persson
Goals: Grahn 90
Uruguay: Mazurkiewicz, Ubinas (c), Ancheta, Matosas, Mujica, Maneiro, Montero Castillo, Cortes, Zubia, Esparrago (Fontes), Losada
Referee: Landauer (USA)

Italy 0-0 Israel
11/07/70 – Toluca (La Bombonera)
Italy: Albertosi, Burgnich, Cera, Rosato, Facchetti (c), Bertini, Mazzola, De Sisti, Domenghini (Rivera), Boninsegna, Riva
Israel: Vissoker, Bar, Rosen, Bello, Primo, Schwager, Rosenthal, Shum, Spiegel, Spiegler (c), Feigenbaum (Rom)
Referee: De Moraes (Brazil)

	Pld	W	D	L	GF	GA	Pts
Italy	3	1	2	0	1	0	4
Uruguay	3	1	1	1	2	1	3
Sweden	3	1	1	1	2	2	3
Israel	3	0	2	1	1	3	2

Italy and Uruguay qualified for quarter-finals.

Group 3

England 1-0 Romania
02/06/70 – Guadalajara (Jalisco)
England: Banks, Newton (Wright), Labone, Moore (c), Cooper, Ball, Mullery, R Charlton, Lee (Osgood), Hurst, Peters
Goals: Hurst 65
Romania: Adamache, Satmareanu, Dinu, Mocanu, Lupescu, Dumitru, Nunweiller, Dembrovschi, Tataru (Neagu), Dumitrache, Lucescu (c)
Referee: Loraux (Belgium)

Brazil 4-1 Czechoslovakia
03/06/70 – Guadalajara (Jalisco)
Brazil: Felix, Carlos Alberto (c), Brito, Piazza (Fontana), Everaldo, Clodoaldo, Gerson (Paulo Cesar), Rivelino, Jairzinho, Tostao, Pelé
Goals: Rivelino 24, Pelé 59, Jairzinho 61, 81
Czechoslovakia: Viktor, Dobias, Horvath (c), Hagara, Migas, Hrdlicka (Kvasnak), Kuna, F Vesely (B Vesely), Petras, Adamec, Jokl
Goals: Petras 11
Referee: Barreto (Uruguay)

Romania 2-1 Czechoslovakia
06/06/70 – Guadalajara (Jalisco)
Romania: Adamache, Satmareanu, Dinu, Mocanu, Lupescu, Dumitru (Gergely), Nunweiller, Dembrovschi, Neagu, Dumitrache, Lucescu (c) (Tataru)
Goals: Neagu 52, Dumitrache pen 75
Czechoslovakia: Vencel, Dobias, Horvath (c), Zlocha, Migas, Kvasnak, Kuna, B Vesely, Petras, Jurkanin (Adamec), Jokl (F Vesely)
Goals: Petras 5
Referee: De Leo (Mexico)

Brazil 1-0 England
07/06/70 – Guadalajara (Jalisco)
Brazil: Felix, Carlos Alberto (c), Brito, Piazza, Everaldo, Clodoaldo, Rivelino, Jairzinho, Tostao (Roberto), Pelé, Paulo Cesar
Goals: Jairzinho 59
England: Banks, Wright, Labone, Moore (c), Cooper, Ball, Mullery, R Charlton (Bell), Lee (Astle), Hurst, Peters
Referee: Klein (Israel)

Brazil 3-2 Romania
10/06/70 – Guadalajara (Jalisco)
Brazil: Felix, Carlos Alberto (c), Brito, Fontana, Everaldo (Marco Antonio), Clodoaldo (Edu), Piazza, Jairzinho, Tostao, Pelé, Paulo Cesar
Goals: Pelé 19, 67, Jairzinho 22
Romania: Adamache (Raducanu), Satmareanu, Dinu, Mocanu, Lupescu, Dumitru, Nunweiller, Dembrovschi, Neagu, Dumitrache (Tataru), Lucescu (c)
Goals: Dumitrache 34, Dembrovschi 84
Referee: Marschall (Austria)

England 1-0 Czechoslovakia
11/06/70 – Guadalajara (Jalisco)
England: Banks, Newton, J Charlton, Moore (c), Cooper, Bell, Mullery, R Charlton (Ball), Peters, Clarke, Astle (Osgood)
Goals: Clarke pen 50
Czechoslovakia: Viktor (c), Dobias, Hrivnak, Hagara, Migas, Pollak, Kuna, F Vesely, Petras, Adamec, Capkovic (Jokl)
Referee: Machin (France)

	Pld	W	D	L	GF	GA	Pts
Brazil	3	3	0	0	8	3	6
England	3	2	0	1	2	1	4
Romania	3	1	0	2	4	5	2
Czechoslovakia	3	0	0	3	2	7	0

Brazil and England qualified for quarter-finals.

Group 4

Peru 3-2 Bulgaria
02/06/70 – Leon (Nou Camp)
Peru: Rubinos, Campos (J Gonzalez), de la Torre, Chumpitaz (c), Fuentes, Mifflin, Challe, Baylon (Sotil), Leon, Cubillas, Gallardo
Goals: Gallardo 50, Chumpitaz 55, Cubillas 73
Bulgaria: Simeonov, Shalamanov, I Dimitrov (c), Penev, Aladzhov, Davidov, Bonev (Asparoukhov), Yakimov, Popov (Marashliev), Zhekov, Dermendzhiev
Goals: Dermendzhiev 13, Bonev 49
Referee: Sbardella (Italy)

West Germany 2-1 Morocco
03/06/70 – Leon (Nou Camp)
West Germany: Maier, Vogts, Schulz, Fichtel, Hottges (Lohr), Haller (Grabowski), Beckenbauer, Overath, Seeler (c), Muller, Held
Goals: Seeler 56, Muller 78
Morocco: Kassou, Lamrani, Khanoussi (c), Slimani, Benkhrif, Mahroufi, Bamous (Faras), El Filali, Ghandi, Ghazouani (El Khiati), Houmane
Goals: Houmane 21
Referee: Van Ravens (Holland)

Peru 3-0 Morocco
06/06/70 – Leon (Nou Camp)
Peru: Rubinos, P Gonzalez, de la Torre, Chumpitaz (c), Fuentes, Mifflin (Cruzado), Challe, Sotil, Leon, Cubillas, Gallardo (Ramirez)
Goals: Cubillas 65, 75, Challe 67
Morocco: Kassou, Lamrani, Khanoussi (c), Slimani, Benkhrif (Fadili), Mahroufi, Bamous, El Filali, Ghandi (Alaoui), Ghazouani, Houmane
Referee: Bakhramov (USSR)

West Germany 5-2 Bulgaria
07/06/70 – Leon (Nou Camp)
West Germany: Maier, Vogts, Schnellinger, Fichtel, Hottges, Seeler (c), Beckenbauer (Weber), Overath, Libuda, Muller, Lohr (Grabowski)
Goals: Libuda 20, Muller 27, pen 52, 88, Seeler 67
Bulgaria: Simeonov, Gaydarski, Zhechev, Penev, Gaganelov (c) (Shalamanov), Nikodimov, Bonev, Kolev, Marashliev, Asparoukhov, Dermendzhiev (Mitkov)
Goals: Nikodimov 12, Kolev 89
Referee: Ortiz de Mendibil (Spain)

West Germany 3-1 Peru
10/06/70 – Leon (Nou Camp)
West Germany: Maier, Vogts, Schnellinger, Fichtel, Hottges (Patzke), Seeler (c), Beckenbauer, Overath, Libuda (Grabowski), Muller, Lohr
Goals: Muller 19, 26, 39
Peru: Rubinos, P Gonzalez, de la Torre, Chumpitaz (c), Fuentes, Mifflin, Challe (Cruzado), Sotil, Leon (Ramirez), Cubillas, Gallardo
Goals: Cubillas 44
Referee: Aguilar (Mexico)

Bulgaria 1-1 Morocco
11/06/70 – Leon (Nou Camp)
Bulgaria: Yordanov, Shalamanov (c), Zhechev, Penev (I Dimitrov), Gaydarski, Kolev, Nikodimov, Yakimov (Bonev), Popov, Asparoukhov, Mitkov
Goals: Zhechev 40
Morocco: Hazzaz, Fadili, Khanoussi (c), Slimani, Benkhrif, Mahroufi, Bamous (Choukri), El Filali, Ghandi, Alaoui (Faras), Ghazouani
Goals: Ghazouani 61
Referee: Ribeiro (Portugal)

	Pld	W	D	L	GF	GA	Pts
West Germany	3	3	0	0	10	4	6
Peru	3	2	0	1	7	5	4
Bulgaria	3	0	1	2	5	9	1
Morocco	3	0	1	2	2	6	1

West Germany and Peru qualified for quarter-finals.

Quarter-finals

At a sweltering Azteca, the **USSR** and **Uruguay** fought a battle of endurance to decide who would reach the semi-finals. The Soviets showed the greater ambition but they struggled to break down the massed Uruguayan defence. The South Americans for their part made little attempt to win the game, seeking to preserve parity until, inevitably, the terrible spectacle was prolonged into extra time. With the intense heat taking its toll on the players, both sides wilted in the added 30 minutes. Ukrainian striker Anatoliy Byshovets thought he'd put the USSR into the lead but the goal was disallowed for offside. The game was drifting towards completing 120 minutes of goalless football and the drawing of lots to decide who would qualify. Then, four minutes from the end, Uruguay substitute Victor Esparrago ensured it would be his side going through, heading in Luis Cubilla's cross from close range. The Soviets protested furiously, as they clearly believed the ball had gone out of play before Cubilla's cross, but the referee was having none of it and replays suggested his decision was correct. Uruguay had won, though in truth the Soviets had probably just been the better of two uninspired sides.

Mexico were forced to leave their base in the capital and travel to the heights of Toluca. Now without their hordes of passionate supporters, they proved no match at all for an **Italy** side unrecognisable from the one which had spluttered through the group stage. Nevertheless, it was the hosts who took the lead, Javier Fragoso's good work setting up Jose Gonzalez to fire past Enrico Albertosi. However, a moment of misfortune gave Italy an equaliser before the break, Angelo Domenghini's shot from the right taking a wicked deflection off Gustavo Pena and creeping past Ignacio Calderon at the near post for a luckless own goal. Italy returned for the second half a different side. The brilliant Gianni Rivera had been brought on in place of Sandro Mazzola and he instantly set about controlling the game. Just past the hour, Luigi Riva did superbly to give the Europeans the lead, collecting a long pass from Giancarlo De Sisti, cutting back past two defenders and rifling into the corner. The crowd were stunned into silence and Rivera dealt them a further blow, seeing his initial effort blocked but keeping his cool in the ensuing goalmouth scramble to finally fire home when presented with a second opportunity. Before the end, the Italians had made it four, breaking quickly on the counterattack and Rivera picking out Riva with a pinpoint pass, allowing the forward to beat Calderon at the second attempt. Italy, having scored just one goal in three group games, had hit four in 90 minutes to extinguish the hosts' challenge.

Guadalajara played host to a thrilling all-South American clash between **Brazil** and **Peru**. The Peruvians, managed by former Brazil great Didi, delighted in taking the game to their more illustrious opponents and the two sides both put the onus on attack in an exceptional match. Pelé saw a thunderbolt free-kick ruled out because it had been awarded as indirect but 11 minutes in Brazil took the lead, Tostao playing another intelligent ball to tee up Rivelino, whose ferocious left-foot shot from out wide on the edge of the area swerved viciously in at the far corner. Four minutes later and the two Brazilian stars swapped roles, Rivelino crossing from the left and Tostao, seeing keeper Luis Rubinos slightly off his line, improbably beating the custodian from the by-line, his shot going almost through Rubinos, who will have been disappointed with conceding such a goal. However, before half-time Alberto Gallardo had pulled one back for Peru in almost identical fashion, his powerful shot from well out on the left beating the hapless Felix even though the keeper was in the right position. Nevertheless, Brazil hit back early in the second half, Pelé seeing his effort palmed away by Rubinos but the lurking Tostao tapping into the empty net to double his tally. Still, though, Peru fought. Teofilo Cubillas, outstanding yet again, deservedly grabbed his fifth goal of the tournament, following in after the Brazilian defence had only partially cleared to smash home a loose ball from the edge of the area. The final word, though, lay inevitably with free-scoring Brazil winger Jairzinho, who got his name on the scoresheet for the fourth successive game, running onto Rivelino's through-ball, rounding Rubinos and sliding the ball in from a tight angle. Peru had certainly played their part in an outstanding contest but no-one could argue that the brilliant Brazilians were anything other than worthy winners.

In a repeat of the 1966 World Cup final, **England** and **West Germany** met at Leon for the last semi-final place. England were dealt a blow before kick-off when star keeper Gordon Banks went down with food poisoning and his understudy Peter Bonetti had to come in in his place. Nevertheless, England were much the better side and for an hour enjoyed total control over their fierce rivals. Keith Newton was exceptional raiding forward from right-back and he created the opener on the half-hour, crossing for England's midfield destroyer Alan Mullery to sweep home. England continued to boss the game in the second half and when Geoff Hurst cleverly played in Newton down the right again, the Everton man's cross was turned in by Martin Peters. 2-0 up and in control, the game looked over. However, England had reckoned without the Germans' legendary fighting spirit. Franz Beckenbauer galvanised them when his shot from the edge of the area squirmed under Bonetti's body, a desperately poor goal to concede and one which Banks would almost certainly have saved. Manager Alf Ramsey's reaction was to remove Bobby Charlton, who was struggling in the heat, in order to save him for the semi-final. However, this move fatally freed Beckenbauer, who had been marking Charlton, and he became more and more influential. Germany managed a shock equaliser when Karl-Heinz Schnellinger put a hopeful ball into the area, Uwe Seeler, with his back to goal, headed it and the ball somewhat fortunately flew into the back of the net. Yet again, extra time would be needed to separate these two teams who were so evenly matched. In the extra 30 minutes, Charlton's replacement, Colin Bell, saw his fine cross headed inches over the bar by Geoff Hurst but it was the Germans' belief against tired opponents that spurred Helmut

Only at the World Cup

England's surprise defeat to the Germans is generally seen as being caused by Banks' enforced absence due to food poisoning, since the usually reliable Bonetti didn't have his best game, and by Ramsey's substitution of Charlton. However, in truth Bonetti was only really at fault for the first goal, while Charlton was clearly struggling late in the game and his replacement Bell played superbly when he came on. Nevertheless, the reputations of Bonetti and Ramsey would never be the same again, while Charlton had played his 106th and last international. Yet more victims of an England failure!

Schon's side on. Substitute right winger Jurgen Grabowski, such a key figure in their revival in the match, flew past Terry Cooper and his deep cross was knocked back across goal by Hannes Lohr where the lurking Gerd Muller volleyed it from point-blank range past an out-of-position Bonetti. England could have equalised at the end but were denied what seemed like a penalty for a foul on Bell and they were heading home. Inevitably it was keeper Bonetti and manager Ramsey who bore the brunt of the English press' assault but in truth they had merely been unlucky against a side whose incredible belief and determination had pulled them back from the brink.

Quarter-final results

USSR 0-1 Uruguay (aet)
14/06/70 – Mexico City (Azteca)
USSR: Kavazashvili, Dzodzuashvili, Khurtsilava (Logofet), Shesternev (c), Afonin, Kaplichny, Asatiani (Kiselev), Muntian, Byshovets, Yevriuzhikin, Khmelnitsky
Uruguay: Mazurkiewicz, Ubinas (c), Ancheta, Matosas, Mujica, Maneiro, Montero Castillo, Cortes, Cubilla, Fontes (Esparrago), Morales (Gomez)
Goals: Esparrago 116
Referee: Van Ravens (Holland)

Italy 4-1 Mexico
14/06/70 – Toluca (La Bombonera)
Italy: Albertosi, Burgnich, Cera, Rosato, Facchetti (c), Bertini, Mazzola (Rivera), De Sisti, Domenghini (Gori), Boninsegna, Riva
Goals: Pena (og) 25, Riva 63, 76, Rivera 70
Mexico: Calderon, Vantolra, Pena (c), Guzman, Perez, Gonzalez (Borja), Pulido, Munguia (Diaz), Valdivia, Fragoso, Padilla
Goals: Gonzalez 13
Referee: Scheurer (Switzerland)

Brazil 4-2 Peru
14/06/70 – Guadalajara (Jalisco)
Brazil: Felix, Carlos Alberto (c), Brito, Piazza, Marco Antonio, Clodoaldo, Gerson (Paulo Cesar), Rivelino, Jairzinho (Roberto), Tostao, Pelé
Goals: Rivelino 11, Tostao 15, 22, Jairzinho 75
Peru: Rubinos, Campos, Fernandez, Chumpitaz (c), Fuentes, Mifflin, Challe, Baylon (Sotil), Leon (Reyes), Cubillas, Gallardo
Goals: Gallardo 28, Cubillas 70
Referee: Loraux (Belgium)

West Germany 3-2 England (aet)
14/06/70 – Leon (Nou Camp)
West Germany: Maier, Vogts, Schnellinger, Fichtel, Hottges (Schulz), Seeler (c), Beckenbauer, Overath, Libuda (Grabowski), Muller, Lohr
Goals: Beckenbauer 68, Seeler 76, Muller 108
England: Bonetti, Newton, Labone, Moore (c), Cooper, Ball, Mullery, R Charlton (Bell), Lee, Hurst, Peters (Hunter)
Goals: Mullery 31, Peters 49
Referee: Coerezza (Argentina)

Uruguay, Italy, Brazil and West Germany qualified for semi-finals.

World Cup Great – Bobby Charlton (England)

The Munich air disaster of February 1958 robbed both Manchester United and England of some great players, in particular wing-half Duncan Edwards. However, one of those who survived would go on to become England's most successful and arguably greatest footballer. His name was Robert "Bobby" Charlton.

Together with older brother Jack, Charlton pursued a football career from a young age and was signed by Manchester United. A highly versatile as well as talented player, he could play as an attacking midfielder, left winger or centre forward and was one of the famed "Busby Babes", a group of extravagantly talented Manchester United players in their early 20s who set about dominating the English game in the late 1950s. However, the Munich air crash killed eight of the team, with Charlton one of the survivors. He was therefore a crucial part of the side's attempts to rebuild following the tragedy.

Soon after the tragic crash, Charlton earned his first England cap at the age of 20, scoring a stunning goal in a victory over Scotland. After an impressive start to his international career he was taken to the 1958 World Cup in Sweden but surprisingly did not play as England went out in the first round. However, by the time of the 1962 tournament, Charlton had firmly established himself as one of the team's stars with a glut of goals from midfield, many of them the spectacular long-range efforts that were his trademark, and started all England's games, playing on the left wing. He enjoyed great success, scoring a thumping effort against Argentina, and was one of the stars of the tournament despite England's quarter-final exit.

By the time of the 1966 World Cup on home soil, the 28-year-old Charlton was indisputably the team's star player, having helped United to a league title in 1965 and starred repeatedly for club and country. It was him who set England on their march to victory with their first goal of the tournament, a stunning solo effort against Mexico, before pulling the strings as England progressed. His best performance of the tournament came in the semi-final win over Portugal, where he scored both goals, one of them another piledriver, to carry England to the final. In the biggest match itself, Charlton was kept relatively quiet by being man-marked by a young Franz Beckenbauer. However, this tactic kept Beckenbauer from influencing the game and gave space to England's other attackers, most notably Geoff Hurst, who scored a hat-trick as England won 4-2. Charlton, one of the tournament's best players, won the European Footballer of the Year award that year in recognition of his importance in the victory.

After such great success for his country, Charlton would go on to enjoy the same at Manchester United. He formed a formidable attacking trio with Northern Ireland winger George Best and Scotland striker Denis Law and this deadly threesome helped United carry off another league title in 1967. The following season, ten years after Munich, would see United achieve the ultimate redemption, winning the European Cup with a 4-1 win over Benfica, Charlton scoring twice to ensure his side were the first English team to win the trophy.

Charlton's international swansong was the 1970 World Cup in Mexico. Aged 32, he was no longer the formidable attacking force he once was, instead playing a deeper role where he effortlessly pulled the strings for his exceptional side. England cruised into the quarter-finals and seemed to be on a march into the final but they lost 3-2 after extra time to West Germany, despite leading 2-0 at one stage. Charlton was controversially substituted after the Germans' first goal and this is often seen as the turning point of the match. However, the reality was that Charlton was tiring in the heat and no longer could keep a check on the rampant Beckenbauer. Nevertheless, defeat brought Charlton's glittering international career to an end. He retired with 106 caps, then an England record, and 49 goals, a record for his country which still stands.

Charlton played on for Manchester United for a further three seasons, finally leaving the club with 748 appearances, a record which Ryan Giggs broke in the 2008 Champions League Final, and 249 goals, which remains unchallenged to this day. After a brief tenure as a player manager at Preston North End, he returned to the club where he had spent almost his entire career to act as a director.

One of the most recognisable footballers of his time, Charlton was balding from his early 20s and famously played with his few strands of hair blowing in the wind as he tried to keep them under check in a comb-over. However, it was his unrivalled ability to score spectacular goals from range that made him a fan favourite. One of England's most versatile and most successful players, Charlton adapted effortlessly to every role he ever played. He is generally considered to be England's greatest ever player, even one of the greatest of any nationality. A true gentleman as well as an outstanding player, Bobby Charlton remains one of the icons of the English game.

World Cup Great – Bobby Moore (England)

The stereotypical English defender is a heavily built, uncompromising figure, powerful in the air and who takes to thumping the ball upfield or out of play whenever in possession. However, the man who ranks unquestionably as England's greatest ever defender, Bobby Moore, was the complete opposite of this model. Not particularly quick and sometimes unsure in the air, Moore's phenomenal reading of the game, perfectly-timed tackling and visionary passing made him one of the first, and best, sweepers of all time, a general conducting his troops from the back.

Moore first appeared for local club West Ham United as a fresh-faced 17-year-old in 1958. His composure and vision at the back instantly made him a fixture in the club's first-team and he would soon be appointed team captain, a position he would retain for the majority of his career. He made his England debut in 1962 and was so impressive he earned a shock place in the squad for the World Cup that year in Chile. Indeed, Moore came from nowhere to be an ever-present at the back, commanding a formidable back-line before England eventually lost to Brazil in the quarter-finals.

At the age of just 22, Moore played his first game as England captain in 1963 and would be permanently given the job the following year. The maturing Moore became a key factor in one of West Ham's most successful ever periods, winning the FA Cup in 1964, the European Cup Winners' Cup in 1965 and losing in the League Cup Final in 1966. By the time of the World Cup on home soil later that year, Moore was firmly installed as the captain and leader of Alf Ramsey's team. He would be the man tasked with leading his troops to triumph.

Moore was at the heart of the side who carried off the trophy in that tournament and was arguably the best player in the competition, leading from the back with calm and assuredness in his own dominant manner. In the final itself, his vision and passing were instrumental in creating two goals for his West Ham colleague Geoff Hurst and as such it was Moore who has the honour of being the only England captain ever to lift the World Cup in triumph. Even at this moment of celebration, Moore's dignity and thoughtfulness were fully exhibited as the great defender, realising his hands were dirty, wiped them on his shorts so as not to muddy the Queen's glove.

After a shock defeat to Yugoslavia in the semi-finals of the European Championships in 1968, Moore and England headed to Mexico in 1970 to defend their World Cup trophy as joint favourites with Brazil. However, before the tournament could kick off, Moore was accused of stealing a bracelet in Colombia and placed under house arrest until he was eventually released and the charges dropped. Nevertheless, he would not let this event ruin his preparations for the tournament and would again be one of England's stars.

Arguably Moore's most memorable performance for England is the first-round game against Brazil. Although England lost 1-0, Moore was exceptional at the back, performing a tackle on Jairzinho frequently considered the greatest tackle of all time. After the game he swapped shirts with the great Pelé, who always held up England's skipper as the fairest and best defender he ever faced, calling him: "My friend, as well as the greatest defender I ever played against." England would eventually lose narrowly to the Germans in the quarter-finals, though their star player, Franz Beckenbauer, would be another glowing in his praise of Moore.

Moore continued to captain England through the qualifiers for the 1974 World Cup. However, England's failure to beat Poland in their final game saw them miss out on a place at the tournament and manager Alf Ramsey was sacked. Moore's final game was a friendly against Italy in 1973. He retired with 108 caps, a record for an England outfield player only broken in 2009 by David Beckham.

Bobby Moore left West Ham in 1974, having set an appearance record since broken only by Billy Bonds, to join fellow London side Fulham. He led his new team to the FA Cup Final in 1975, where he faced old employers West Ham. This time, Moore could not enjoy one last hurrah as the Hammers claimed victory. Moore played out his final years in the fledgling North American Soccer League, retiring in 1978.

Tragically, Moore died suddenly of bowel cancer in 1993, leaving a nation in mourning. His famous number six shirt has since been retired by West Ham, who have also named a stand after him and erected a statue of him with his World Cup club team mates Hurst and Martin Peters. England's greatest ever captain and defender, the great Bobby Moore vies with Beckenbauer for the title of the world's greatest defender and team mate Bobby Charlton for the accolade of England's greatest ever player.

World Cup Great – Gordon Banks (England)

Though Soviet great Lev Yashin is almost unanimously considered the greatest goalkeeper of all time, there is one other player who is sometimes considered to be his equal and possibly even his better. That man is England's legendary custodian Gordon Banks.

Banks first joined Chesterfield, the club he supported as a boy, as a 17-year-old in 1955. After impressing there for several seasons, he was snapped up by Leicester City in 1959. His performances for his new club earned him a call-up for the 1962 World Cup, though he was only understudy to Ron Springett for the tournament. However, the following year he was given his first cap by new coach Ramsey and went on to become England's first-choice keeper for almost a decade.

By the 1966 World Cup, Banks was one of the stars of the England team. In his prime, he was all but unbeatable, keeping four successive clean sheets before Eusebio finally beat him from the penalty spot in the semi-final. Although, he let in two goals in the final against the Germans, England scored four to win the World Cup for the first time. They had much to thank Banks for.

Just a year later, Banks left Leicester City after a young Peter Shilton, who would later succeed him as England keeper, made his name coming through the club's youth ranks. England's number one joined Stoke City, where he enhanced his reputation and was still his country's undisputed first choice for the 1970 World Cup. Against Brazil in that tournament he produced the "save of the century", brilliantly throwing himself to the ground to tip a bullet header from Pelé over the bar. The goal he conceded to Jairzinho later in the game would be the only one he let in all tournament. However, Banks went down with food poisoning before the quarter-final with West Germany. In his absence, England lost 3-2, with his understudy Peter Bonetti at fault.

Banks remained England's undisputed number one for the next two years until in October 1972 he was involved in a car accident which destroyed the sight in his right eye. Since this massively hampered his goalkeeping, Banks was unable to continue as a player, going into scouting before a brief return to playing football in the North American Soccer League from 1977-78.

Although Shilton was a superb goalkeeper and England number one for the best part of two decades, Banks is still considered unanimously to be England's greatest ever goalkeeper and is generally regarded the world over as the second best keeper ever after Yashin. He could not match Yashin's innovations or ability at saving penalties but Banks was unmatched in his positioning and shot-stopping abilities. As important as any player in the 1966 World Cup win and in the brilliant side of 1970, Gordon Banks will forever rank as a true England great.

Semi-finals

At Guadalajara, **Brazil** faced another all South American clash, this time meeting **Uruguay** in a classic case of defence versus attack. However, the game did not pan out exactly as expected. Uruguay started surprisingly brightly and promptly took the lead when Julio Morales superbly played in Luis Cubilla to beat Felix and put his side in front. The match then deteriorated greatly as a spectacle, with countless fouls from both sides disrupting the rhythm of the game. Brazil took to brutally bringing down Cubilla to limit the darting winger's impact, while Uruguay retreated into massed defence to protect their lead. However, just before the break, midfielder Clodoaldo burst forward, played a slick one-two with Tostao and ran on to slot past Ladislao Mazurkiewicz. In the second period, Pelé almost scored what would have been one of the most audacious goals ever seen. Racing onto a through-ball, his outrageous dummy completely baffled onrushing keeper Mazurkiewicz, as the great number 10 simply allowed the ball to run past him instead of taking a touch. Sadly, Pelé didn't have the luck to go with such breathtaking skill, his shot drifting inches wide of the open goal. It wasn't to matter, however, as inevitably Jairzinho got his customary goal some 14 minutes from time, a scintillating passing move resulting in Tostao playing the winger through and he kept his cool to sprint clear of the defence and tuck the ball past Mazurkiewicz. At the death, Rivelino crowned Brazil's performance with a fine

Only at the World Cup

Pelé produced an outrageous piece of skill to fox Uruguay keeper Mazurkiewicz. He ran onto a through-ball but, instead of trying to knock the ball past the keeper, he dummied to take a touch but instead ran around the keeper while letting the ball continue on its path. Mazurkiewicz was utterly beaten but sadly for Pelé he somehow managed to shoot wide of the now open goal.

third, racing onto Pelé's lay-off and smashing a wicked left-foot effort into the corner. Brazil's dream team were in the final.

In one of the greatest games of football ever played, European giants **Italy** and **West Germany** met at the Azteca to decide who would play Brazil in the World Cup final. After just eight minutes, Roberto Boninsegna seized on a hesitant clearance from the German defence, picking his spot and shooting in accurately from the edge of the area. It looked like Italy would progress comfortably, strengthened further by the introduction of Gianni Rivera at half-time. Their cause was aided when Franz Beckenbauer fell heavily and injured his shoulder; with both permitted substitutions already used, the Bayern Munich man was forced to play on with his arm in a sling. However, with seconds remaining, the Germans conjured an improbable equaliser, Jurgen Grabowski's cross clipped home by defender Karl-Heinz Schnellinger, an unsung hero of this great German side. The match would go to extra time. As against England, the Germans' late equaliser gave them the momentum and they scored a scrappy goal to take the lead, Gerd Muller seizing on hesitancy in the Italian defence to nudge the ball past Enrico Albertosi and see it creep over the line. Facing elimination, the Italians conjured up a mighty effort and hit back. Right-back Tarcisio Burgnich popped up in the box to divert a lofted free-kick past Sepp Maier and then just before half-time in extra time, Angelo Domenghini found Luigi Riva and the Cagliari star fired accurately into the corner. Italy were back in front and seemingly on the way to the final. However, even now the Germans refused to give up. Naturally it was little poacher Muller who rescued them again, profiting from Uwe Seeler's knock-down to turn in his tenth goal

Only at the World Cup

Italy's dramatic semi-final meeting with West Germany is known in several languages as the "game of the century" and is widely considered the greatest football match of all time. The Germans equalised in the final minute of normal time and in a seesaw additional 30 minutes, five goals were scored as the lead switched between both teams before the Italians eventually prevailed 4-3.

of the tournament, all scored from inside the box, and level things up once again. The Germans celebrated wildly but incredibly they were behind again just a minute after Muller's equaliser. With determination, Italy marched their way up the field as the Germans fatally took their eye off the ball. Boninsegna pulled back and it was Rivera, making another convincing statement for a starting spot, who was there to fire in the winner. Amazingly, Italy had triumphed 4-3 after extra time, finally breaking the Germans' heroic resistance and fighting spirit. It would be the Azzurri who would participate in their third World Cup final.

Semi-final results

Uruguay 1-3 Brazil
17/06/70 – Guadalajara (Jalisco)
Uruguay: Mazurkiewicz, Ubinas (c), Ancheta, Matosas, Mujica, Maneiro (Esparrago), Montero Castillo, Cortes, Cubilla, Fontes, Morales
Goals: Cubilla 19
Brazil: Felix, Carlos Alberto (c), Brito, Piazza, Everaldo, Clodoaldo, Gerson, Rivelino, Jairzinho, Tostao, Pelé
Goals: Clodoaldo 44, Jairzinho 76, Rivelino 89
Referee: Ortiz De Mendibil (Spain)

Italy 4-3 West Germany (aet)
17/06/70 – Mexico City (Azteca)
Italy: Albertosi, Burgnich, Cera, Rosato (Poletti), Facchetti (c), Bertini, Mazzola (Rivera), De Sisti, Domenghini, Boninsegna, Riva
Goals: Boninsegna 8, Burgnich 98, Riva 104, Rivera 111
West Germany: Maier, Vogts, Schnellinger, Schulz, Patzke (Held), Seeler (c), Beckenbauer, Overath, Grabowski, Muller, Lohr (Libuda)
Goals: Schnellinger 90, Muller 94, 110
Referee: Yamasaki (Peru)

Brazil and Italy qualified for final, Uruguay and West Germany to third-place play-off.

World Cup Great – Uwe Seeler (West Germany)

Germany has produced a host of world-class strikers during its time as a football superpower but Uwe Seeler was probably the first to gain entrance to this club. A mainstay of the national team for more than 15 years, Seeler was a prolific scorer, a committed worker and a born leader.

Seeler came up through the ranks of his home club Hamburg, which he joined when he was still a boy. At the age of 18 in 1954 he made his debut for the club's senior side and marked the occasion with a hatful of goals. Before the year was out he had also made his debut for the national team, who had won their first World Cup against the odds months earlier. In 1958, Seeler was one of the youngsters brought in to freshen up the side in their title defence. This move had the desired effect, as the Germans again resembled the team who had caused such a stir in 1954. 21-year-old Seeler was a key part of the revival, the young centre forward scoring twice and looking a constant threat as the champions eventually bowed out in the semi-finals.

Back at Hamburg, Seeler's reputation was growing with every game he played and the young star helped his side to the title in 1960, winning the German Footballer of the Year award for his achievements. He was an integral part of the German side in the 1962 World Cup, though around him much of the team was being rebuilt, resulting in a disappointing quarter-final exit. Nevertheless, Seeler managed to bag two more World Cup goals and further enhance his reputation as one of Europe's most feared strikers.

With the retirement of Hans Schafer, Seeler took over the captaincy of the national team, combining it with captaining Hamburg. He was the top scorer of the inaugural Bundesliga season in 1964 with 30 goals, ensuring he was again voted German Footballer of the Year. These achievements set him up well for his third World Cup, 1966, and his first as captain. Again he was one of the tournament's best forwards, scoring twice to lead his team to the final, the only time Seeler would play in the biggest international match of all. Sadly for him, he could not prevent hosts England winning 4-2 after extra time. Indeed, the image of a distraught Seeler walking off after the game is among the most iconic in German football history.

Seeler would have one final shot at the World Cup in 1970, when, aged 33, he dropped back to captain his team from the midfield, alongside Franz Beckenbauer and Wolfgang Overath. In that tournament he and Pelé became the first players to score in four different World Cups before Seeler set himself clear as the first to score at least twice in four different tournaments – only Miroslav Klose has since matched him. The Hamburg star scored his third of the tournament and ninth career World Cup goal against England in the quarter-final, a crucial equaliser before his successor at centre forward, Gerd Muller, fired an extra-time winner. However, Seeler's side bowed out to Italy in an incredible semi-final. Nevertheless, Seeler's appearance in the third-place play-off against Uruguay was his 21st World Cup match, then a record but since surpassed by compatriot Lothar Matthaus.

After being named German Footballer of the Year a third time in 1970, Seeler retired from football in 1972, having spent his entire career with Hamburg. One of the greatest strikers of his era, Seeler was blessed with superb technical ability as well as unshakeable belief and determination. Dominant in the air and a fine finisher off either foot, Seeler was also famous for his ability at the bicycle kick, one of the most technically demanding moves in football. A tremendously popular character on and off the pitch, Uwe Seeler was a credit to German football.

Third-place Play-off

Before the main event of the final, **Uruguay** and **West Germany** sought to lift themselves from the pain of elimination by achieving the small consolation of third place. The Uruguayans seemed to treat the game the more seriously of the two, playing their strongest available line-up and showing surprising ambition for a team with a reputation for negativity. The Germans, meanwhile, made several changes, including the enforced absence of the injured Beckenbauer. Unsurprisingly, they were exhausted due to the demands of extra time in both their previous games. Nevertheless, their incredible will to win, even for so hollow a victory as this, lifted them to give it their all and incredibly they prevailed, one of their remaining stars, midfield playmaker Wolfgang Overath, scoring the only goal. The Germans had deservedly claimed the bronze medal but the Uruguayans could also be proud of their own fine campaign.

Third-place Play-off result

Uruguay 0-1 West Germany
20/06/70 – Mexico City (Azteca)
Uruguay: Mazurkiewicz, Ubinas (c), Ancheta, Matosas, Mujica, Maneiro (Sandoval), Montero Castillo, Cortes, Cubilla, Fontes (Esparrago), Morales
West Germany: Wolter, Vogts, Schnellinger (Lorenz), Fichtel, Patzke, Seeler (c), Weber, Overath, Libuda (Lohr), Muller, Held
Goals: Overath 26
Referee: Sbardella (Italy)

West Germany claimed third place.

World Cup Final

The ninth World Cup final, at Mexico City's Azteca stadium, came with an extra incentive: whichever of **Brazil** and **Italy** were victorious would seal a third World Cup win and would be allowed to keep the Jules Rimet trophy permanently in recognition of the achievement. Both sides stuck with the same line-ups who had won their semi-finals, meaning Italy's star Gianni Rivera was again left on the bench. The final was expected to see Brazil's attack pitted against Italy's defence but if sitting back had been the Azzurri's game plan then it was in tatters after 18 minutes as Brazil took the lead. A throw-in on the left flank was collected by Rivelino and he floated in a cross for Pelé, the striker using exquisite timing to rise above Giacinto Facchetti at the far post and head his 12th World Cup goal in four tournaments, just one behind Just Fontaine's record. The Italians were forced to chase the game and they were gifted a route back into the match with eight minutes left before half-time. For all Brazil's attacking talent, they had a tendency to go to sleep at the back and this time it was midfielder Clodoaldo who was the guilty party. Without looking he attempted to perform a cross-field back-heel but striker Roberto Boninsegna intercepted the ball, shrugged off defender Brito's attempt to block him, rounded keeper Felix and rolled the ball into the empty net.

Brazil and the crowd, who were firmly backing the South Americans, were stunned and Italy were in the ascendancy.

In the second half, Brazil continued to attack but try as they might could not breach Italy's resolute defence. Pelé was inches away from connecting with Carlos Alberto's cross at the far post while Rivelino struck a thunderous right-foot free-kick against the bar but still they could not regain the lead. However, midway through the half, they finally found the goal the stadium craved. Left-back Everaldo gave the ball to Jairzinho and though the winger's jinking run was blocked off, the ball fell for midfield orchestrator Gerson, who stepped past a defender, picked his spot and crashed the ball into the corner for an exceptional goal, his first of the tournament. Gerson was pulling the strings expertly in midfield, given time on the ball to produce his inch-perfect passes, and it was he who made the game safe for Brazil five minutes later. Out wide on the left by the halfway line, Gerson floated a fabulous pass into the area, Pelé used his chest to cushion the ball into the path of Jairzinho and the Botafogo man poked the ball past Enrico Albertosi to ensure he had scored at least once in every game of the tournament. Brazil's football was breathtaking and the Italians were left chasing shadows by the end of the game. With four minutes remaining, the South Americans delivered the coup de grace with arguably the greatest goal ever scored in a World Cup. Tostao intercepted the ball deep in his own half, passed to defender Piazza and the ball flowed through Clodoaldo, Pelé and Gerson before Clodoaldo showed off his dribbling skills, tormenting the Italians as he weaved his way round four of them before finding Rivelino out wide. Rivelino pumped the ball forward to Jairzinho, whose step-over and run pulled the Italian defence out of position, and the winger found Pelé on the edge of the area. Showing incredible vision, the world's best player paused before rolling the ball to his right, where captain Carlos Alberto was bursting forward to smash a thunderous effort across Albertosi and into the far corner. The roof almost came off the stadium and at the final whistle the jubilant crowd invaded the pitch as the Brazilians celebrated wildly. It was all too much for Rivelino, who passed out from the emotion of it all, while fans tore Pelé's shirt from his back. Carlos Alberto and his team paraded the Jules Rimet Trophy around the stadium. He would be the last captain ever to hold it above his head to celebrate World Cup victory.

Stat Attack

Jairzinho became the fourth player, after Sarosi, Ghiggia and Fontaine, to score in every match of a World Cup.

Stat Attack

Victory allowed Pelé and coach Mario Zagallo to set individual records. Pelé is the only man ever to win the World Cup three times as a player as well as one of only four to score three goals in finals and to score in two different finals, while Zagallo became the first man to win the World Cup both as a player and as a manager.

Only at the World Cup

Winning the tournament allowed Brazil to keep the Jules Rimet Trophy permanently. However, it was stolen in 1983 and was never recovered. It is believed that the thieves melted it down and, sadly, the original figure of Nike with arms aloft in victory will never be seen again.

World Cup Final result

Brazil 4-1 Italy
21/06/70 – Mexico City (Azteca)
Brazil: Felix, Carlos Alberto (c), Brito, Piazza, Everaldo, Clodoaldo, Gerson, Rivelino, Jairzinho, Tostao, Pelé
Goals: Pelé 18, Gerson 66, Jairzinho 71, Carlos Alberto 86
Italy: Albertosi, Burgnich, Cera, Rosato, Facchetti (c), Bertini (Juliano), Mazzola, De Sisti, Domenghini, Boninsegna (Rivera), Riva
Goals: Boninsegna 37
Referee: Glockner (East Germany)

Brazil won the 1970 World Cup.

Tournament awards

Golden Boot: Gerd Muller (West Germany) – 10 goals
(Runner-up: Jairzinho (Brazil) – 7)

Best Player: Pelé (Brazil)

Best Goal: Carlos Alberto (Brazil) – Considered by many the greatest ever World Cup strike, the so-called "President's Goal" in the final against Italy was the ultimate team goal. Building from the back, Brazil constructed a brilliant passing move between eight players (defenders Brito and Everaldo were the only outfield players not to touch the ball) featuring a magical dribble from Clodoaldo and ending in Pelé's lay-off and Carlos Alberto's thumping first-time finish. Sublime.

Star XI:
Goalkeeper – Gordon Banks (England)
Defenders – Carlos Alberto (Brazil), Atilio Ancheta (Uruguay), Bobby Moore (England), Giacinto Facchetti (Italy)
Midfielders – Franz Beckenbauer (West Germany), Gerson (Brazil), Roberto Rivelino (Brazil)
Forwards – Jairzinho (Brazil), Gerd Muller (West Germany), Pelé (Brazil)

World Cup Great – Pelé (Brazil)

How does anyone begin to talk about the great Pelé? The greatest footballer, possibly even the greatest sportsman the world is ever likely to see, Pelé was the complete player. There was nothing he couldn't do on the football field, while off it he is revered as the global ambassador for what he describes as the "beautiful game".

Born Edson Arantes do Nascimento as the son of a footballer, Pelé grew up in poverty and his parents discouraged him from taking up the game. However, they could not stop Pelé, who had such a genuine passion for the game that he would play with grapefruits, since he was too poor to afford a proper ball. Spotted by Waldemar de Brito, a member of the 1934 World Cup squad, he was made known to Sao Paulo club Santos, who signed him as a 15-year-old in 1956. He made his club debut that same year, scoring in his first match. In the 1957 season, the 16-year-old became an overnight superstar, becoming his team's key player and scoring more goals than any other player in the league, receiving his first Brazil cap before his 17th birthday as a mark of his brilliant performances. In that match he scored his first international goal aged 16 years and less than nine months, an incredible statistic.

By the time of the 1958 World Cup, the then 17-year-old had played his way into Vicente Feola's squad. He was not initially a first-choice but Brazil's poor performances in their first two games saw Pelé introduced, making him at the time the youngest ever World Cup player. Pelé instantly turned Brazil's fortunes around with a string of exceptional performances, becoming the youngest ever World Cup goalscorer against Wales, notching a hat-trick against France and scoring twice in the final, once with an exceptional piece of skill, to make himself the youngest ever player and scorer in a final. It was quite a glittering array of personal accolades for a teenage boy.

Over the next few years, Pelé set about establishing himself as the premier footballer in the world and this was a title he most certainly held by the time of the 1962 World Cup in Chile. Now 21, Pelé announced his arrival in the tournament with a magical solo goal against Mexico. However, he suffered an injury in the next game against Czechoslovakia and missed the rest of the tournament. Brazil went on to win but significantly of Pelé's three World Cup triumphs this is the one thought of in the least glamorous fashion. Yes the Brazil 1962 side were a fine team but they were missing that spark of individual genius that Pelé would have provided.

By this time the vultures were circling Santos as the cream of European club football battled to take the star number ten away from his home country. However, so highly did Brazil value Pelé that the country's government actually put a ban on a potential transfer abroad. Pelé for his part was more than happy to remain at Santos and continued to bang in the goals and turn in fabulous performances. He travelled to the 1966 World Cup in England as the unquestioned star of the Brazil team. However, the rest of the side was in a rebuilding process, mixing ageing veterans from the previous two triumphs with talented but untested youngsters. In the end, they couldn't find their feet and went out in the first round. What is most notable about Brazil's participation in the tournament, however, was the shocking treatment awarded to Pelé. The great forward scored against Bulgaria with a free-kick but spent the rest of the game being savagely kicked into submission, receiving an injury which forced him out of the defeat to Hungary. He returned for the crunch match with Portugal only to receive even more shocking treatment, culminating in a scandalous challenge from Morais that left him a limping passenger.

After the horrors of 1966, Pelé vowed never to play in another World Cup. However, the appointment of 1958 and 1962 team mate Mario Zagallo as manager changed his mind and he would go on to be the star of the tournament in 1970. 29 and in his prime, Pelé roamed along the forward line, listed as a striker but frequently dropping deep to orchestrate play. He scored four goals in the tournament, including one in the final, to take his tally to 12 World Cup goals, a Brazilian record until broken by Ronaldo 36 years later. However, it was his irresistible all-round play, incredible vision and breathtaking skill for which he is best remembered. He came agonisingly close to scoring two goals which would have ranked among the best ever in World Cups, a lob from his own half against Czechoslovakia and an outrageous dummy against Uruguay. Pelé's best performance of all came in the final itself, scoring once and setting up two more while utterly dominating the game. Famously, Italy right-back Tarcisio Burgnich said of him after the match: "I told myself before the game, 'He's made of skin and bones just like everyone else'. But I was wrong."

Pelé played his final game for Brazil a year later. He was still just 30 and could well have played for many years to come but his legacy as the game's greatest ever player was already complete. He left with a phenomenal record of 77 goals in 92 caps, making him the third most prolific international scorer of all time and the top scorer in the history of the Brazilian national team. He continued to star off and on with Santos until 1974, winning five titles in a row and scoring well over a thousand goals, making him the top goalscorer of all time.

In 1975, Pelé decided to see out the final years of his career in the North American Soccer League, where he played for New York Cosmos. His arrival instantly swelled interest in the game in the USA, where it has so often had to fight for popularity against traditional American sports. The King's final ever match came days before his 37th birthday in October 1977, a testimonial against the Santos side he had been the central part of for almost 20 years. It was a fitting tribute to the career of the club's greatest ever player.

Pelé remains a highly visible and influential figure in the world of football today. He is the game's number one ambassador to the world, his combination of incredible footballing ability, humility and gentlemanly conduct making him perfect for the job. A great man as well as a great player, Pelé's name will always be synonymous with his "beautiful game." Pelé will always remain The King and it is unlikely there will ever be another to match football's greatest ever player. His skill set was complete and he could do everything effortlessly on the field. He combined supreme ball skills, vision, passing, trickery, composure, thunderous shooting ability off either foot, phenomenal ability in the air and time on the ball with the physical attributes of lightning pace and robust physical strength. Every other player of the game has been weak in one area but not Pelé. The incomparable Pelé, the sport's great man, the King of football, will forever remain number one.

After the terrible physical brutality of the two tournaments of the 1960s, thankfully the World Cup of 1970 saw a return in the large part to the free-flowing, attacking football of the 1950s. The game had obviously become far more defensive since then but the general attitude of teams was much more positive, the skill levels were considerably higher and, most importantly, violence and negative play were noticeable by their absence. Indeed, not a single player was sent off in the tournament.

There can be little doubt that the irresistible Brazilians were worthy champions. With the incomparable Pelé at the absolute peak of his powers and a formidable supporting cast including the free-scoring Jairzinho, the orchestrator Gerson, the composed Rivelino and the little general Tostao, the South Americans simply blew away every opponent they faced. Indeed, some consider the 1970 Brazil side to be the greatest team of all time. Certainly, they are up there with the very best, although the 1958 side were probably a more balanced unit and were certainly stronger in defence.

Nevertheless, there is no doubt that no side has ever lit up a World Cup to the same extent as Pelé and co did in Mexico 1970.

If there was one sour point from the neutrals' perspective it would have been that the Brazilians did not face England in the final. Clearly the next best team in the tournament and much stronger than their 1966 winning side, Alf Ramsey's men were exceptional in every match they played, the only team to really challenge Brazil, and surely would have reached the final had Gordon Banks not been forced out of the quarter-final with food poisoning. With that slight element of doubt in the back of their minds, perhaps that was why West Germany were able to come back from the dead to win. The Germans too were an exceptional side, even better than their 1966 vintage. With Franz Beckenbauer now a mature and commanding presence and Gerd Muller a prolific marksman, they had an exceptional tournament and in their semi-final with Italy they took part in probably the greatest match in the tournament's history. The Italians too for their part had impressed at times, most notably in that incredible match against the Germans. However, they had been no match at all for Brazil in the final. Quite why reigning European Footballer of the Year Gianni Rivera barely played in the tournament is a mystery, especially considering his exceptional performances whenever he did get on the pitch.

Overall, 1970 was a glowing success. Widely considered the greatest World Cup of them all (though some of the 1950s tournaments definitely run it close) it was packed with brilliant attacking football, glorious goals, great sides and some of the world's greatest ever players. It was the ultimate advert for the game of football.

1974: West Germany

Qualification

99 Entrants.
Brazil qualified as holders.
West Germany qualified as hosts.

Europe

Group 1

Malta 0-2 Hungary, Austria 4-0 Malta, Hungary 3-0 Malta, Sweden 0-0 Hungary, Austria 2-0 Sweden, Austria 2-2 Hungary, Sweden 7-0 Malta, Malta 0-2 Austria, Hungary 2-2 Austria, Sweden 3-2 Austria, Hungary 3-3 Sweden, Malta 1-2 Sweden

	Pld	W	D	L	GF	GA	Pts
Sweden	6	3	2	1	15	8	8
Austria	6	3	2	1	14	7	8
Hungary	6	2	4	0	12	7	8
Malta	6	0	0	6	1	20	0

Play-off (in West Germany): Sweden 2-1 Austria

Sweden qualified.

Group 2

Luxembourg 0-4 Italy, Switzerland 0-0 Italy, Luxembourg 2-0 Turkey, Turkey 3-0 Luxembourg, Italy 0-0 Turkey, Turkey 0-1 Italy, Italy 5-0 Luxembourg, Luxembourg 0-1 Switzerland, Switzerland 0-0 Turkey, Switzerland 1-0 Luxembourg, Italy 2-0 Switzerland, Turkey 2-0 Switzerland

	Pld	W	D	L	GF	GA	Pts
Italy	6	4	2	0	12	0	10
Turkey	6	2	2	2	5	3	6
Switzerland	6	2	2	2	2	4	6
Luxembourg	6	1	0	5	2	14	2

Italy qualified.

Group 3

Belgium 4-0 Iceland, Iceland 0-4 Belgium (in Belgium), Norway 4-1 Iceland, Norway 0-2 Belgium, Holland 9-0 Norway, Belgium 0-0 Holland, Iceland 0-4 Norway, Holland 5-0 Iceland, Iceland 1-8 Holland (in Holland), Norway 1-2 Holland, Belgium 2-0 Norway, Holland 0-0 Belgium

	Pld	W	D	L	GF	GA	Pts
Holland	6	4	2	0	24	2	10
Belgium	6	4	2	0	12	0	10
Norway	6	2	0	4	9	16	4
Iceland	6	0	0	6	2	29	0

Holland qualified.

Group 4

Finland 1-0 Albania, Finland 1-1 Romania, East Germany 5-0 Finland, Romania 2-0 Albania, East Germany 2-0 Albania, Albania 1-4 Romania, Romania 1-0 East Germany, Finland 1-5 East Germany, East Germany 2-0 Romania, Albania 1-0 Finland, Romania 9-0 Finland, Albania 1-4 East Germany

	Pld	W	D	L	GF	GA	Pts
East Germany	6	5	0	1	18	3	10
Romania	6	4	1	1	17	4	9
Finland	6	1	1	4	3	21	3
Albania	6	1	0	5	3	13	2

East Germany qualified.

Group 5

Wales 0-1 England, England 1-1 Wales, Wales 2-0 Poland, Poland 2-0 England, Poland 3-0 Wales, England 1-1 Poland

	Pld	W	D	L	GF	GA	Pts
Poland	4	2	1	1	6	3	5
England	4	1	2	1	3	4	4
Wales	4	1	1	2	3	5	3

Poland qualified.

Group 6

Portugal 4-0 Cyprus, Cyprus 0-1 Portugal, Bulgaria 3-0 Northern Ireland, Cyprus 0-4 Bulgaria, Cyprus 1-0 Northern Ireland, Northern Ireland 1-1 Portugal (in England), Bulgaria 2-1 Portugal, Northern Ireland 3-0 Cyprus (in England), Northern Ireland 0-0 Bulgaria (in England), Portugal 2-2 Bulgaria, Portugal 1-1 Northern Ireland, Bulgaria 2-0 Cyprus

	Pld	W	D	L	GF	GA	Pts
Bulgaria	6	4	2	0	13	3	10
Portugal	6	2	3	1	10	6	7
Northern Ireland	6	1	3	2	5	6	5
Cyprus	6	1	0	5	1	14	2

Bulgaria qualified.

Group 7

Spain 2-2 Yugoslavia, Yugoslavia 1-0 Greece, Greece 2-3 Spain, Spain 3-1 Greece, Yugoslavia 0-0 Spain, Greece 2-4 Yugoslavia

	Pld	W	D	L	GF	GA	Pts
Spain	4	2	2	0	8	5	6
Yugoslavia	4	2	2	0	7	4	6
Greece	4	0	0	4	5	11	0

Play-off (in West Germany): Spain 0-1 Yugoslavia

Yugoslavia qualified.

Group 8

Denmark 1-4 Scotland, Scotland 2-0 Denmark, Denmark 1-1 Czechoslovakia, Czechoslovakia 6-0 Denmark, Scotland 2-1 Czechoslovakia, Czechoslovakia 1-0 Scotland

	Pld	W	D	L	GF	GA	Pts
Scotland	4	3	0	1	8	3	6
Czechoslovakia	4	2	1	1	9	3	5
Denmark	4	0	1	3	2	13	1

Scotland qualified.

Group 9

France 1-0 USSR, Republic of Ireland 1-2 USSR, Republic of Ireland 2-1 France, USSR 1-0 Republic of Ireland, France 1-1 Republic of Ireland, USSR 2-0 France

	Pld	W	D	L	GF	GA	Pts
USSR	4	3	0	1	5	2	6
Republic of Ireland	4	1	1	2	4	5	3
France	4	1	1	2	3	5	3

USSR qualified for UEFA/CONMEBOL play-off.

South America

Group 1

Colombia 1-1 Ecuador, Colombia 0-0 Uruguay, Ecuador 1-1 Colombia, Ecuador 1-2 Uruguay, Uruguay 0-1 Colombia, Uruguay 4-0 Ecuador

	Pld	W	D	L	GF	GA	Pts
Uruguay	4	2	1	1	6	2	5
Colombia	4	1	3	0	3	2	5
Ecuador	4	0	2	2	3	8	2

Uruguay qualified.

Group 2

Bolivia 1-2 Paraguay, Argentina 4-0 Bolivia, Paraguay 1-1 Argentina, Bolivia 0-1 Argentina, Paraguay 4-0 Bolivia, Argentina 3-1 Paraguay

	Pld	W	D	L	GF	GA	Pts
Argentina	4	3	1	0	9	2	7
Paraguay	4	2	1	1	8	5	5
Bolivia	4	0	0	4	1	11	0

Argentina qualified.

Group 3

Venezuela withdrew.
Peru v Chile: 2-0, 0-2 (agg. 2-2), Play-off (in Uruguay): Chile 2-1 Peru

Chile qualified for UEFA/CONMEBOL play-off.

UEFA/CONMEBOL Play-off

USSR v Chile: 0-0, USSR refused to play return leg and were disqualified.

Chile qualified.

> ### Only at the World Cup
>
> Chile were scandalously allowed to host their play-off game in the Estadio Nacional, where dictator Augusto Pinochet had been torturing political opponents to death. The USSR unsurprisingly boycotted the game, giving Chile a spot in the finals.

North and Central America

Preliminary Round

Group 1

Canada 3-2 USA, Canada 0-1 Mexico, USA 2-2 Canada, Mexico 3-1 USA, Mexico 2-1 Canada, USA 1-2 Mexico

	Pld	W	D	L	GF	GA	Pts
Mexico	4	4	0	0	8	3	8
Canada	4	1	1	2	6	7	3
USA	4	0	1	3	6	10	1

Mexico qualified for final round.

Group 2

Guatemala v El Salvador: 1-0, 1-0 (agg. 2-0)

Guatemala qualified for final round.

Group 3

Honduras v Costa Rica: 2-1, 3-3 (agg. 5-4)

Honduras qualified for final round.

Group 4

Jamaica withdrew.

Dutch Antilles qualified for final round.

Group 5

Haiti v Puerto Rico: 7-0, 5-0 (agg. 12-0)

Haiti qualified for final round.

Group 6

Trinidad and Tobago 11-1 Antigua and Barbuda, Antigua and Barbuda 1-2 Trinidad and Tobago, Trinidad and Tobago 2-1 Dutch Guiana, Dutch Guiana 1-1 Trinidad and Tobago (in Trinidad), Antigua and Barbuda 0-6 Dutch Guiana, Dutch Guiana 3-1 Antigua and Barbuda (in Antigua)

	Pld	W	D	L	GF	GA	Pts
Trinidad and Tobago	4	3	1	0	16	4	7
Dutch Guiana	4	2	1	1	11	4	5
Antigua and Barbuda	4	0	0	4	3	22	0

Trinidad and Tobago qualified for final round.

Final Round (in Haiti)

Honduras 2-1 Trinidad and Tobago, Mexico 0-0 Guatemala, Haiti 3-0 Dutch Antilles, Honduras 1-1 Mexico, Haiti 2-1 Trinidad and Tobago, Guatemala 2-2 Dutch Antilles, Haiti 1-0 Honduras, Mexico 8-0 Dutch Antilles, Trinidad and Tobago 1-0 Guatemala, Dutch Antilles 2-2 Honduras, Haiti 2-1 Guatemala, Trinidad and Tobago 4-0 Mexico, Guatemala 1-1 Honduras, Trinidad and Tobago 4-0 Dutch Antilles, Haiti 0-1 Mexico

	Pld	W	D	L	GF	GA	Pts
Haiti	5	4	0	1	8	3	8
Trinidad and Tobago	5	3	0	2	11	4	6
Mexico	5	2	2	1	10	5	6
Honduras	5	1	3	1	6	6	5
Guatemala	5	0	3	2	4	6	3
Dutch Antilles	5	0	2	3	4	19	2

Haiti qualified.

Africa

First Round

Algeria v Guinea: 1-0, 1-5 (agg. 2-5)
Lesotho v Zambia: 0-0, 1-6 (agg. 1-6)
Togo v Zaire: 0-0, 0-4 (agg. 0-4)
Dahomey v Ghana: 0-5, 1-5 (agg. 1-10)
Kenya v Sudan: 2-0, 0-1 (agg. 2-1)
Nigeria v Congo: 2-1, 1-1 (agg. 3-2)
Sierra Leone v Ivory Coast: 0-1, 0-2 (agg. 0-3)
Morocco v Senegal: 0-0, 2-1 (agg. 2-1)
Tanzania v Ethiopia: 1-1, 0-0 (agg. 1-1), Play-off (in Ethiopia): Ethiopia 3-0 Tanzania
Egypt v Tunisia: 2-1, 0-2 (agg. 2-3)
Madagascar v Mauritius: Madagascar withdrew, Mauritius received bye.
Gabon v Cameroon: Gabon withdrew, Cameroon received bye.

Guinea, Zambia, Zaire, Ghana, Kenya, Nigeria, Ivory Coast, Morocco, Ethiopia, Tunisia, Mauritius and Cameroon qualified for second round.

Second Round

Mauritius v Kenya: 1-3, 2-2 (agg. 3-5)
Cameroon v Zaire: 0-1, 1-0 (agg. 1-1), Play-off (in Zaire): Zaire 2-0 Cameroon
Nigeria v Ghana: 0-2 (match abandoned, Ghana awarded win), 0-0 (agg. 0-2)
Guinea v Morocco: 1-1, 0-2 (agg. 1-3)
Tunisia v Ivory Coast: 1-1, 1-2 (agg. 2-3)
Ethiopia v Zambia: 0-0, 2-4 (agg. 2-4)

Kenya, Zaire, Ghana, Morocco, Ivory Coast and Zambia qualified for third round.

Third Round

Ivory Coast v Morocco: 1-1, 1-4 (agg. 2-5)
Ghana v Zaire: 1-0, 1-4 (agg. 2-4)
Zambia v Kenya: 2-0, 2-2 (agg. 4-2)

Morocco, Zaire and Zambia qualified for final round.

Final Round

Zambia 4-0 Morocco, Zambia 0-2 Zaire, Zaire 2-1 Zambia, Morocco 2-0 Zambia, Zaire 3-0 Morocco, Morocco withdrew before game with Zaire, 0-2 Zaire awarded.

	Pld	W	D	L	GF	GA	Pts
Zaire	4	4	0	0	9	1	8
Zambia	4	1	0	3	5	6	2
Morocco	4	1	0	3	2	9	2

Zaire qualified.

Asia and Oceania

India, Philippines and Sri Lanka withdrew before draw was made.

Zone A (in South Korea)

South Vietnam 1-0 Thailand, Israel 2-1 Japan, Hong Kong 1-0 Malaysia

South Vietnam, Japan and Hong Kong to Group One, Thailand, Israel and Malaysia to Group Two.

Group 1

Japan 4-0 South Vietnam, Hong Kong 1-0 Japan, Hong Kong 1-0 South Vietnam

	Pld	W	D	L	GF	GA	Pts
Hong Kong	2	2	0	0	2	0	4
Japan	2	1	0	1	4	1	2
South Vietnam	2	0	0	2	0	5	0

Hong Kong and Japan qualified for zonal semi-finals.

Group 2

South Korea 4-0 Thailand, Israel 3-0 Malaysia, South Korea 0-0 Malaysia, Israel 6-0 Thailand, South Korea 0-0 Israel, Malaysia 2-0 Thailand

	Pld	W	D	L	GF	GA	Pts
Israel	3	2	1	0	9	0	5
South Korea	3	1	2	0	4	0	4
Malaysia	3	1	1	1	2	3	3
Thailand	3	0	0	3	0	12	0

Israel and South Korea qualified for zonal semi-finals.

Semi-finals

South Korea 3-1 Hong Kong, Israel 1-0 Japan (aet)

South Korea and Israel qualified for zonal final.

Final

South Korea 1-0 Israel (aet)

South Korea qualified for play-off with Zone B winner.

Zone B

Group 1 (in Iran)

Iran 0-0 North Korea, Syria 2-1 Kuwait, Iran 2-1 Kuwait, North Korea 1-1 Syria, Iran 1-0 Syria, North Korea 0-0 Kuwait, Iran 2-1 North Korea, Syria 2-0 Kuwait, Iran 2-0 Kuwait, North Korea 3-0 Syria, Iran 0-1 Syria, Kuwait 2-0 North Korea

	Pld	W	D	L	GF	GA	Pts
Iran	6	4	1	1	7	3	9
Syria	6	3	1	2	6	6	7
North Korea	6	1	3	2	5	5	5
Kuwait	6	1	1	4	4	8	3

Iran qualified for zonal final.

Group 2 (in Australia)

Australia 1-1 New Zealand, Australia 3-1 Iraq, New Zealand 1-1 Indonesia, Australia 2-1 Indonesia, Iraq 2-0 New Zealand, Australia 3-3 New Zealand, Iraq 1-1 Indonesia, Australia 0-0 Iraq, Indonesia 1-0 New Zealand, Iraq 3-2 Indonesia, Australia 6-0 Indonesia, Iraq 4-0 New Zealand

	Pld	W	D	L	GF	GA	Pts
Australia	6	3	3	0	15	6	9
Iraq	6	3	2	1	11	6	8
Indonesia	6	1	2	3	6	13	4
New Zealand	6	0	3	3	5	12	3

Australia qualified for zonal final.

Final

Australia v Iran: 3-0, 0-2 (agg. 3-2)

Australia qualified for play-off with Zone A winner.

Zonal Play-off

Australia v South Korea: 0-0, 2-2 (agg. 2-2)
Play-off (in Hong Kong): Australia 1-0 South Korea

Australia qualified.

The Contenders

Argentina   Italy
Australia   Poland
Brazil   Scotland
Bulgaria   Sweden
Chile   Uruguay
East Germany   West Germany
Haiti   Yugoslavia
Holland   Zaire

The tenth World Cup, hosted by West Germany, had the added attraction of a new trophy, the imaginatively named FIFA World Cup Trophy, as Brazil's third triumph in 1970 had allowed them to keep the Jules Rimet Trophy permanently. The Germans would be hosting their second major international tournament in two years, as Munich had been the host of the Olympic Games in 1972. That competition had been most notable for the tragic murder of several Israeli athletes and so security would be very much to the fore in the World Cup. Sadly, this would not make for the best of atmospheres for the fans but it was impossible to dispute that the safety of the competitors was the most important thing of all.

For this tournament, the competition format had changed for the first time since 1958. Instead of a knockout system from the quarter-finals onwards, the eight teams progressing from their groups would be drawn in two further groups, the winners of which would contest the final outright. However, optimism ahead of the tournament was low and not only because of fears about the heavy levels of security. Several of the traditional powerhouses of the international game, particularly the Western European nations such as England, France and Spain, had failed to qualify for the tournament, which would lack their large numbers of passionate fans. At least some of the teams and players present looked capable of offsetting this disappointment.

Group One was based in West Berlin and Hamburg and hosts and seeds **West Germany** were expected to progress from it with ease. Helmut Schon's side had been unstoppable in sweeping all before them to win the 1972 European Championship and their squad was so strong that that team's star man, attacking midfielder Gunter Netzer, couldn't get past Wolfgang Overath into the starting line-up. With captain Franz Beckenbauer effortlessly controlling the game from his new sweeper position, Sepp Maier redoubtable in goal, Berti Vogts a terrier in defence and Gerd Muller prolific as ever up front, they looked like mounting a serious challenge for the title.

Intriguingly, one of their first-round opponents would be **East Germany**, first-time qualifiers, and their clash with their western neighbours would be dominated by political undertones. The two nations' relations were strained to say the least and the match-up between the two sides would be laced with emotion. For their part, the East Germans came with an impressive side, certainly not of the same level as the West, but a dangerous outfit nonetheless. Striker Joachim Streich was a real goal threat while Jurgen Croy was one of the very best goalkeepers in the world. They certainly came with at least a chance of leaving an impact on their neighbours' tournament.

Chile, boasting such a dismal record in Europe, came hoping to make it out of the first round of the World Cup for the first time since finishing third on home soil in 1962. They had benefited from the USSR's play-off withdrawal, while in centre-back Elias Figueroa they had one of the top players in all of South America. Nevertheless, getting one over the two German sides in their group would be no easy task.

The final side in the group would be **Australia**, making their World Cup bow and the first side from their continent to make it to football's biggest tournament. Just happy to be at the party, their chances of making it any further in the competition looked incredibly slim. Still, their army of loud and passionate supporters would certainly enjoy the occasion and would do their best to liven up the atmosphere at the tournament.

Mario Zagallo's **Brazil** headed up Group Two, which would be played out in Frankfurt, Gelsenkirchen and Dortmund. The reigning champions had lost many of the players who had been so impressive in the march to glory in 1970, most notably the great Pelé, while his able strike partner Tostao had been forced into early retirement with an eye injury. Still, in playmaker Rivelino they had a player with one of the best left-foots in the business and the free-scoring winger Jairzinho would be back to assist him in the creative department. However, fearing the physicality of the European game, the beautiful football the Selecao played in 1970 had largely been abandoned in favour of a more defensive, rugged game, where keeper Emerson Leao and centre-back Luis Pereira would be key figures. However, for the neutrals, Brazil would not be half as fun to watch.

Keeping them company would be a fine **Yugoslavia** team who had talent running throughout their squad. A defence anchored by Ivan Buljan and Josip Katalinski gave freedom to a multi-talented midfield of Branko Oblak and flying winger Dragan Dzajic, who the English press had nicknamed "Magic Dragan" after a sublime performance in the 1968 European Championships. With a good blend of youth and experience, not to mention incredible talent, they looked a real prospect.

Scotland too came with a highly capable side that had the potential to have a major say in tournament proceedings. Manchester United legend Denis Law may have been 34 but on his day he was still a quality striker while youngster Kenny Dalglish looked a formidable prospect alongside him. The likes of Jimmy Johnstone and Peter Lorimer were exceptional wide men, Billy Bremner a ferocious pitbull of a holding midfielder while Martin Buchan and Danny McGrain would hold the fort together at the back. Everything looked in place for a major challenge.

The fourth side in the group would be an unknown quantity in **Zaire**, the first African side not from the Arabic north of the country to reach the World Cup finals. Their qualifying form had been impressive, including winning all four of their matches in the final round of their qualifying tournament, but the standard of football was about to take a massive leap. Whether or not the Leopards could compete would be a matter of great interest to those watching around the globe.

Group Three would take place in Hanover, Dusseldorf and Dortmund and would be headed up by **Holland**, seen by many as overwhelming favourites for the title. Coach Rinus Michels had invented the concept of "Total Football" in his time at Ajax, a system whereby every player was able to cover any position on the pitch, the left midfielder, for example, dropping into left-back if the left-back went on a forward run – every player both attacked and defended. With this system, Dutch sides had cleaned up honours at European level, Feyenoord winning the European Cup in 1970 before Ajax won it three seasons in a row in 1971, 1972 and 1973. The star of that side, European Footballer of the Year on two of those occasions (1971 and 1973), was Holland's talisman Johan Cruyff, now at Barcelona and the best player in the world. A centre forward by name, Cruyff in actuality could play almost anywhere and do almost anything and had the world at his feet. Assisting him were a slew of fabulously gifted players: full-backs Wim Suurbier and Ruud Krol, midfield powerhouse Johan Neeskens and wingers Johnny Rep and Piet Keizer were all former team mates of Cruyff at Ajax, while Rob Rensenbrink starred up front for Anderlecht and the likes of midfielders Wim Jansen and Wim Van Hanegem were exceptional for Feyenoord. Oddly, with so much talent available, Michels' side had only just qualified for the tournament ahead of neighbours Belgium but now they were there they were determined to make their mark. Widely tipped to carry off the trophy despite having never even got out of the first round of a World Cup before or even reached the tournament for 36 years, nevertheless they looked all but unstoppable, though significantly an Ajax side shorn of Cruyff had failed to win the European Cup a fourth successive time, the title instead going to West Germany's Bayern Munich, perhaps suggesting a shift of power. All the same, Cruyff and co would take some stopping in the tournament.

The seeded side in the group were **Uruguay**, always impressive performers at World Cup level. However, their side appeared to have fallen into decline after their superb performances in 1970 and they were not a side of the quality of years gone by. The likes of Luis Cubilla and Pedro Rocha were now veterans and keeper Ladislao Mazurkiewicz, in his third tournament, would likely be a busy man, especially given the quality of the Dutch attack. At least striker Fernando Morena was a fine addition.

Sweden arguably looked like presenting the Dutch with a tougher obstacle. Play-off victors over Austria, several of the side had gained their first World Cup experience in 1970 and now would look to build on it. Ronnie Hellstrom in goal, Bjorn Nordqvist at the back, Bo Larsson in midfield and Ove Kindvall up front had all been present in Mexico, while striker Ralf Edstrom looked a new and dangerous prospect. Playing neat, attacking football, they could be a threat.

Bulgaria were the fourth side in the group and had qualified impressively but their hopes had been dealt a severe blow by the tragic death of star striker Georgi Asparoukhov in a car accident. In his absence they would rely heavily on their solid defence, including the battle-hardened Dimitar Penev, as well as the skill of midfielder Hristo Bonev as they searched for their first win at the finals.

Down in the south at Munich and Stuttgart would be Group Four, where **Italy**, runners-up in 1970, had been seeded. They boasted an exceptional side. Goalkeeper Dino Zoff incredibly hadn't let in an international goal since 1972, a run of almost 1,100 minutes of football. Veterans Tarcisio Burgnich and Giacinto Facchetti returned to help guard his goal while Romeo Benetti would be a new and formidable barrier in midfield. In the creative department, Sandro Mazzola and Gianni Rivera remained and might be finally played together this time, while up front Luigi Riva would as ever present a formidable goal threat. The Azzurri certainly looked like being major challengers.

Joining the Italians would be Olympic champions **Poland**, a hugely talented side who had reached only their second World Cup ahead of England in qualifying. However, as glorious as that victory had been, it had cost the Poles the services of star striker Wlodzimierz Lubanski, injured by a Roy McFarland challenge. Nevertheless, Andrzej Szarmach was a more than able deputy and wingers Grzegorz Lato and Robert Gadocha would give him support out wide and in the goalscoring department. The team's real ace, however, looked to be playmaker Kazimierz Deyna, while Wladyslaw Zmuda was a promising young defender and keeper Jan Tomaszewski had been Poland's hero in earning the draw away at England that had sealed qualification. Their country's best ever generation, Poland looked like potential dark horses.

Argentina too would compete in this tough group. Still boasting veteran Roberto Perfumo to keep them secure at the back, the rest of the team was based around an exciting crop of youngsters. These included attacking midfielder Rene Houseman, the dangerous Carlos Babington and teenage striker Mario Kempes, who looked a tremendous prospect. Hosting the competition in 1978, they would want their players to pick up the best possible experience to be able to mount a serious title challenge on home soil four years later.

Lastly came debutants **Haiti**, who looked to have no chance against three sides of such quality as their opponents in Group Four. Qualification for them had been helped by the 1973 CONCACAF Championship, which doubled as the final stage of World Cup qualifiers for the region, being staged on their island. All the same, they would now face a mighty task to save themselves from humiliation, though they would certainly look most of all to enjoy themselves and in striker Emmanuel Sanon they at least had a capable marksman.

Debutants: Australia, East Germany, Haiti, Zaire

The Draw

Group 1
West Germany
Chile
Australia
East Germany

Group 2
Brazil
Yugoslavia
Scotland
Zaire

Group 3
Uruguay
Holland
Bulgaria
Sweden

Group 4
Italy
Haiti
Argentina
Poland

Venues:
Munich, Dortmund, Dusseldorf, Frankfurt, Gelsenkirchen, Hamburg, Hanover, Stuttgart, West Berlin

The Tournament – 13 June-7 July

Group Stage – First Series

The tournament opened in Frankfurt, with holders **Brazil** looking to exhibit their newfound defensive solidity to contain **Yugoslavia**. Sadly for the neutrals, both sides erred very much on the side of caution and the game quickly deteriorated into a sorry spectacle. There was none of the trademark attacking flair from the South Americans, with the Yugoslavs far more prepared to take the initiative. The Europeans had much the better of the game but their attacks floundered against the massed ranks of the Brazilian defence and they were reduced largely to half-chances. Finishing 0-0, it didn't promise much for the tournament ahead.

The next day in Berlin, hosts **West Germany** got their tournament underway against **Chile**. The limited South Americans proved the perfect opponents for the Germans to play themselves into form, offering very little going forward and allowing the hosts to probe in attack. Nevertheless, the Germans could only muster a single goal in their unimpressive 1-0 win, though that was a phenomenal 35-yard thunderbolt from roaming left-back Paul Breitner which flew into the top corner after a sweeping move. The Chileans never threatened a comeback and forward Carlos Caszely compounded their misery by getting himself sent off. However, it was the Germans who were most firmly under the microscope and they would have to improve.

> ### Stat Attack
>
> Chile's Carlos Caszely was the first player to receive a red card in a World Cup (though many before him had been sent off).

Elsewhere in Group One, **East Germany** and **Australia** both made their World Cup debuts, both looking to crown the occasion with victory. Unsurprisingly it was the Germans who dominated, midfielder Jurgen Sparwasser blasting a powerful shot from range just over early on. However, in the second half East Germany did take the lead but in comical circumstances. A through-ball sent Sparwasser racing clear but Jack Reilly was out of goal quickly to force him to attempt to roll the ball in at the far corner. However, before

the ball could get there, defender Colin Curran, back-pedalling, managed to slice his attempted clearance straight into the back of the net. Behind in such a poor fashion, to their credit the Socceroos didn't capitulate, though star striker Joachim Streich did double the Germans' lead before the end, brilliantly stretching to fire Eberhard Vogel's left-wing cross into the top corner. East Germany had matched their western neighbours with a win in their opening game.

At Dortmund's Westfalenstadion, **Scotland** played their first World Cup match in 16 years, with **Zaire**, the first sub-Saharan African team to reach the finals, their opponents. A totally unknown quantity, no-one expected the African debutants to stand a chance against a formidable Scotland side. However, they held out for much of the first period, no doubt aided by Scotland's wasteful finishing. Nevertheless, eventually the Scots did score a goal to settle their nerves, big striker Joe Jordan employing his height advantage to head back across goal and the lurking Peter Lorimer, a dangerous presence roaming across the front line all game, smashing in a trademark thunderbolt volley. Minutes later it was two, the Zaire defence going utterly to sleep when Billy Bremner's right-wing free-kick was swung in, Jordan running forward as the Africans stood still, assuming he was offside, to head beyond keeper Mwamba Kazadi. Scotland should have run riot against tiring opponents in the second period but again they failed to take their chances against the desperately poor Leopards. Scotland had the all-important opening win but they had failed to steal a march on their group rivals by filling their boots with goals.

The tournament had started with a series of dull matches dominated by negative football but the arrival of **Holland** was to change all this. Exhibiting the breathtaking movement and speed of their "Total Football" the Dutch masters tore **Uruguay** to shreds and could easily have scored ten. As it was, they sated themselves with just two, both scored by right winger Johnny Rep, first heading in a Wim Suurbier cross before tapping in a cut-back from Rob Rensenbrink, who had been selected at left wing ahead of Piet Keizer. However, it was the brilliant Johan Cruyff who particularly caught the eye, changing positions all round him and dissecting the Uruguayan defence with his breathtaking movement, vision and passing. The South Americans, humiliated by opponents they simply couldn't win the ball off, inevitably resorted to violence to stop the darting Dutch. Captain and centre-back Juan Carlos Masnik disgracefully escaped punishment for horribly jumping on the ankle of his tormentor Johan Neeskens, while Julio Montero Castillo was dismissed after squaring up to Rensenbrink. Not even these ugly scenes, however, could take anything away from the glorious football of the men in orange, who looked all but unstoppable.

Sadly, the glorious performance of Holland was not a marker as to the football played elsewhere. In the same Group Three, **Sweden** and **Bulgaria** played out a boring and horribly negative 0-0 draw in Dusseldorf. The Swedes at least made some efforts to attack but these were quickly stifled by the Bulgarians' tendency to defend in depth. The Scandinavians lacked the quality to break down these massed ranks, while Bulgaria for their part showed no ambition to go in search of a win.

At Munich's Olympiastadion, Group Four kicked off with what looked like a simple opener for **Italy** against the minnows of **Haiti**. However, they were unable to take the lead by half-time, main striker Luigi Riva guilty of missing a series of simple chances. Straight after the break, the

Haitians punished their opponents for their wastefulness. Midfielder Philippe Vorbe played an exquisite through-ball for Emmanuel Sanon, who incredibly rounded keeper Dino Zoff and slotted into the net. The crowd went wild and Italy faced the very real prospect of being on the receiving end of a shock to match their humbling at the hands of North Korea eight years earlier. However, Sandro Mazzola took it upon himself to haul his team back. Causing havoc wherever he appeared, it was the veteran playmaker who swung over a cross from the right and though the Haitian defence knocked the ball away from Giorgio Chinaglia, Gianni Rivera was in the right place to smash home the equaliser. Italy continued to press and took the lead just past the hour, Romeo Benetti's drive from the edge of the area taking an unfortunate deflection off Arsene Auguste and going in. Italy scored a third before the end, the hapless Riva unable to control Mazzola's visionary pass but substitute striker Pietro Anastasi, who had wasted a golden opportunity minutes earlier, firing home for 3-1. Italy had won but Haiti had worried them throughout and proved themselves deserved qualifiers.

Stuttgart saw **Poland** and **Argentina** play out a thrilling encounter, showcasing football of the highest quality. The Poles were out of the blocks the quicker and made their early dominance count with two quick goals in the opening minutes. The first was gifted to the Europeans by a horrible mistake from Argentine keeper Daniel Carnevali, who jumped to collect a corner but dropped it at the feet of right winger Grzegorz Lato, who tucked it away. Barely a minute later, Lato broke clear and played an incisive through-ball for striker Andrzej Szarmach, who fired accurately beyond Carnevali's reach. The Poles could have gone in at the break further ahead had Szarmach's powerful free-kick not come back off the post. Seconds after the kick-off of the second period, Szarmach again struck the woodwork with a powerful effort as the Poles continued to dominate. However, on the hour Argentina clicked into gear, a neat move seeing Miguel Brindisi, Rene Houseman and Mario Kempes combine to set up centre-back Ramon Heredia to cut back and fire into the corner. However, only two minutes later Poland had a third, little Lato seizing on a loose pass to burst forward and beat Carnevali again. A constant menace, the diminutive winger was proving a real handful. However, Argentina soon hit back in this seesaw encounter, Jan Tomaszewski performing heroically in a goalmouth scramble but Carlos Babington eventually poking the ball in. This prompted a late rally from the South Americans but the Poles held on to claim a deserved win. They had served notice to the rest that they too were an exceptional side.

Group Stage – Second series

West Germany, in front of their passionate fans at Hamburg, predictably had too much in the tank for **Australia**, though to their credit the Socceroos fought manfully and troubled the hosts on several occasions. Nevertheless, they never looked particularly likely to score and were punished three times by the Germans' ruthless finishing. First, just 12 minutes in, Wolfgang Overath picked up a loose ball 25 yards from goal and slammed an unstoppable effort into the top corner. Before the break it was two, the impressive Uli Hoeness tearing down the right flank and planting his cross on the head of Bernd Cullmann. Inevitably it was Gerd Muller, the best goalscorer of them all, who made sure of victory early in the second half, losing his marker to head in Hoeness' corner. The hosts had secured their passage through to the second round but were still to find their best form.

Back in Berlin, **East Germany** were playing just a matter of miles away from the border with their own country as they faced **Chile**. However, they struggled to break down the South Americans and showed limited ambition going forward. Eventually, ten minutes into the second half, Peter Ducke swung in a corner, Martin Hoffmann jumped with the keeper and managed to head the ball past him to score. Nevertheless, the Germans were unable to hold their lead to the finish, poor defending from a Chilean counterattack allowing Carlos Reinoso to cross and Sergio Ahumada to slide in and beat keeper Jurgen Croy. East Germany had been poor and would still have work to do to reach the next stage.

In Group Two, **Scotland** looked to continue their winning start to the competition against champions **Brazil**. The South Americans were the better side in the first period, Leivinha crashing a powerful shot off the crossbar. However, the Scots ran riot in the second half, tormenting the flat-footed Brazilian defence, and they were desperately unlucky not to beat the holders. David Hay and Peter Lorimer, perhaps realising the vulnerability of shaky Brazil keeper Emerson Leao, tested him with frequent long-range shots. However, it was the aerial threat of Joe Jordan that really unsettled the custodian, one knock-down spilled by Leao and the onrushing Billy Bremner, exceptional all game, somehow shooting wide. With that, Scotland's chance was gone. Holding the reigning champions to a 0-0 draw was certainly a fine achievement but their level of domination was such they really should have won.

At Gelsenkirchen, **Zaire**'s hopes came crashing down in a blaze of reality as they were on the end of an almighty humbling at the hands of **Yugoslavia**. The Leopards had learnt just days before they would receive no money for their participation in the tournament and clearly their minds were on other things. The Yugoslavs, a slick attacking side anyway, needed no second invitation to lay waste to the abysmal Africans. Just eight minutes in, Dragan Dzajic burst down the left flank and crossed for Dusan Bajevic to score the first. Dzajic himself got on the scoresheet minutes later, thumping a free-kick into the top corner when the Zaire wall lined up in completely the wrong place. Striker Ivica Surjak was the next to feast on Zaire's dismal defending, a neat team move ending in Jovan Acimovic putting him clear and he comfortably slotted home. Zaire's coach, Yugoslavian Blagoja Vidinic, responded by bringing his keeper Mwamba Kazadi off the field and just 21 minutes had been played! This eccentric decision did little good, as his replacement, Dimbi Tubilandu, was beaten seconds after coming on, Josip Katalinski smashing in Ivan Buljan's cross from the right. Zaire's misery was soon compounded

when Mulumba Ndaye was sent off and they were two more goals down at half-time. First, Ilija Petkovic tore down the right flank and squared for Bajevic to notch his second of the game. Then, after Zaire failed to clear from a corner, Dzajic swung the ball back in, Katalinski jumped with the keeper and centre-back Vladislav Bogicevic rose to head in. With the score 6-0 at half-time, this was already a thrashing of unimaginable proportions. The carnage continued after the break, Tubilandu somehow letting Branko Oblak's free-kick from way out creep past him into the far corner. Minutes later Bajevic raced clear and though he was scythed down horribly on the edge of the area, Petkovic swept home the loose ball. Bajevic would complete his hat-trick before the end, Dzajic swinging in a cross from the left, Acimovic heading on and the Velez Mostar forward firing in at the far post to complete a 9-0 demolition of the hapless Africans, rendering all goal difference calculations academic in a downpour of goals.

Uruguay and **Bulgaria** were both renowned for their attention to defence and their occasionally brutal tactics so there was no surprise that their meeting was full of cynical fouls and precious little attacking football or entertainment. Still, with 15 minutes to go, Bulgaria's captain Hristo Bonev provided the game with inspiration, flying through the air to meet Voin Voinov's cross with a spectacular diving header and the Bulgarians were minutes away from their first World

Cup victory. Uruguay, with elimination seemingly imminent, left it late to equalise, just three minutes remaining when Victor Esparrago picked out the run of left-back Ricardo Pavoni and the defender finished with a fantastically cool effort low into the far corner. Bulgaria had been denied, though a draw was probably a fair reflection of the balance of play.

Holland, meanwhile, failed to beat **Sweden** despite the best efforts of Cruyff and his attacking accomplices. By far the better side, still the Dutch failed to fashion any real openings against a side who fought hard. Strangely given the 0-0 scoreline, the match was one of the better games at the tournament, with both teams concentrating on attack whenever in possession. However, the defences were on top form and neither could be breached. A point would have to do.

> ## Only at the World Cup
>
> Johan Cruyff gave probably the best example of his legendary "Cruyff turn" against Sweden. The Dutch maestro's drag-back was sublime and he produced the trick so quickly that Swede Bo Larsson can be seen facing the wrong way as Cruyff sprints away!

Two of the game's biggest names, **Italy** and **Argentina**, faced one another in Stuttgart. Predictably, the Argentineans looked to attack with flair while Italy sought to sit back and hit the South Americans on the counterattack. It was Argentina's strategy that paid early dividends, Carlos Babington playing through Rene Houseman to give them the lead. However, the luckless Roberto Perfumo was to cost his side the win with an unfortunate own goal before the break. 1-1 would have to do for both sides and it meant both could still harbour ambitions of reaching the second round.

> ## Only at the World Cup
>
> Morale in the Haitian camp was understandably low after the treatment given to Ernst Jean-Joseph after the defender failed a drug test. Officials from the Haitian government, a brutal dictatorship, were not understanding, dragging the player from his hotel room, savagely beating him and extraditing him from the country!

Down in Munich, poor **Haiti** barely escaped the ravages that had been handed out the previous day to Zaire as they were battered 7-0 by **Poland**. Allegations of drug abuse had emerged just before the game, with centre-back Ernst Jean-Joseph the guilty party. The player himself had been brutally dealt with by government officials and morale in the camp was obviously at rock bottom. The Poles took full and ruthless advantage and were already five goals to the good at the break. First, defender Antoni Szymanowski knocked the ball into the path of Grzegorz Lato, who shrugged off a defender's feeble attempt at a clearance and drove the ball home. A minute later, slack marking at a corner allowed Robert Gadocha to swing the ball in and Kazimierz Deyna, the creator of much of the carnage to come, to head home. On the half-hour, the Haitian defence again went to sleep at a corner, allowing Andrzej Szarmach this time to head in Gadocha's ball at the far post. Just seconds later 3-0 had become 4-0 thanks to a truly staggering goal. Poland were awarded a free-kick some 40 yards out, Gadocha rolled the ball to Jerzy Gorgon and the big defender blasted a rocket of a shot into the top corner, almost bursting the net! Three minutes later another swift attack saw Lato play the perfect ball for Szarmach to control and double his personal tally for the game. There was no let-up after the break and Szarmach again exploited Haiti's hesitancy at defending corners to head in Gadocha's swinging ball and bag himself a simple hat-trick. Poland relaxed after that but there was one more goal to come before the end, Szarmach returning the favour to Lato, setting up the winger to lash home. Haiti were humiliated while Poland had only underlined that they were a formidable attacking side.

Group Stage – Third series

The game everyone had been waiting for took place on the 22nd June in Hamburg as hosts **West Germany** met neighbours and political rivals **East Germany**. The West were much the better team and dominated the first half, Gerd Muller hitting the post with a turn and shot while seemingly endless pressure was applied on the East's goal. However, East Germany striker Hans-Jurgen Kreische had the best chance of the half, somehow blazing over from three yards out with the goal at his mercy. The spectacle deteriorated in the second period as the West failed to apply the same level of pressure, while

the East continued to put their emphasis on defence. Then, against the run of play, Erich Hamann's lofted pass picked out midfielder Jurgen Sparwasser, who skipped past a defender and fired high into the roof of the net. Incredibly, unfancied East Germany had won to top the group while the hosts faced the wrath of their supporters. However, although the defeat will have hurt bitterly, all was certainly not lost, as finishing second in the group actually seemed to give West Germany a much kinder second-round draw than their neighbours.

Meanwhile, **Chile** and **Australia** were playing for pride in Berlin. Surprisingly, it was the Australians who were the more attacking of the two, the South Americans again a disappointment. Nevertheless, a first World Cup goal eluded the Socceroos, though in holding Chile to a 0-0 draw they did achieve a point in their debut tournament, even after midfielder Ray Richards was sent off in comical circumstances late on.

In Group Two, **Yugoslavia** and **Scotland** looked for the win that would guarantee them progress to the second round. The Scots, as against Brazil, were much the better side for the majority of the game. Joe Jordan had a golden opportunity to give them the lead in the first half after a defensive slip but keeper Enver Maric was out quickly to smother the shot at his feet. Then, with less than ten minutes remaining, Yugoslavia

took a shock lead with a close-range finish from striker Stanislav Karasi. However, the Scots refused to give up and with seconds remaining a sweeping team move culminated in Tommy Hutchison's cross from the left working its way to Jordan at the far post, who buried his shot in the net. Scotland had their draw but as the final whistle blew, they were waiting for news from Brazil's clash with Zaire, knowing that the Brazilians had to beat the Africans by more than two goals to deny them.

At Gelsenkirchen, **Brazil** were seeking a goalfest against **Zaire** to ensure their own qualification. The Africans, meanwhile, were desperate to save some face after their humiliation at the hands of the Yugoslavs. However, with just 12 minutes gone, Jairzinho swept home from the edge of the area and they were heading for defeat. In the second half, the Leopards sought to stop the South Americans by any means necessary, including right-back Ilunga Mwepu smashing a Brazilian free-kick back down the field and receiving a yellow card for his troubles. Brazil would break through eventually, Rivelino thundering a trademark power drive into the top corner from 25 yards out. Still, though, they needed one more to deny the Scots. With ten minutes to play, it finally arrived, though it was more out of a horrendous goalkeeping error from Kazadi, restored in place of Tubilandu, than from Brazilian skill. Space was worked for Valdomiro on the right but the forward's weak shot was aimed straight at Kazadi, who was covering his near post. However, the keeper somehow let the ball trickle through him and into the back of the net. With that, Brazil had just scraped through, while poor Scotland, who had played much better than the holders over their three games, were on their way home. If only they had been able to take their chances in all three matches.

Back in Group Three, **Holland** again showed their tremendous attacking ability, making mincemeat of **Bulgaria**. The Eastern Europeans, as was their way, soon realised they were no match for the Dutch and so resorted to fouling them. However, the result was that Johan Neeskens twice smashed in unstoppable penalties to put Holland two up at the break. Despite the frequent fouls from both sides, the Dutch were still able to thrill with their breathtaking football. They scored a third goal when Bulgaria failed to clear from a free-kick and Johnny Rep rammed the ball in. The Bulgarians at least were going down fighting and they pulled a goal back when Ruud Krol inadvertently put a left-wing cross into his own net in an attempt to clear. Still, the last word was inevitably Dutch, the indefatigable Johan Cruyff swinging in a cross from the left and substitute Theo De Jong stooping to guide a diving header past Stefan Staikov.

Sweden joined Holland in the second round courtesy of victory over **Uruguay** in Dusseldorf. The Swedes, whose previous two games had both ended in goalless draws, looked like playing out another lifeless encounter after the first 45 minutes passed with almost nothing of incident. However, straight from the second-half kick-off, the Swedes advanced forward and Ove Kindvall squared for Ralf Edstrom to control and smash a powerful half-volley past Ladislao Mazurkiewicz. The Uruguayans, behind and heading home, resorted sadly to violent challenges. It was not enough to stem the tide, however. Kindvall put Roland Sandberg through on the counterattack and the striker raced clear to slot a pinpoint shot just inside the post. Three minutes later and 2-0 had become 3-0. Uruguay gave the ball away sloppily and Sandberg burst away down the flank, unselfishly squaring for Conny Torstensson who in turn offloaded for Edstrom to slip the ball beyond Mazurkiewicz. The Swedes' willingness to attack had finally borne fruit and they would play in the second round.

Argentina, knowing that goal difference could well be important in deciding who qualified from Group Four, sought to beat **Haiti** convincingly to give themselves the best chance of progressing. Predictably, with Haiti still recovering from the trauma of their hammering by the Poles, the islanders let in two quick goals from Hector Yazalde and the exceptional attacking midfielder Rene Houseman, the latter laid on by Yazalde. In the second half, little striker Ruben Ayala added a third from Enrique Wolff's ball before Haiti got a consolation, the Argentinean defence desperately clearing a dangerous attack but Emmanuel Sanon collecting the loose ball 25 yards out and blasting it gloriously into the top corner. Yazalde capped his impressive performance by notching his second soon after, however, and Argentina were easy winners 4-1. By the end, though, they were more concerned with news from Stuttgart, where they knew they would go through if Italy lost to Poland.

Poland had already sealed qualification and so **Italy** were hoping they might take their foot off the gas somewhat and allow the Azzurri to claim the point they needed to progress. However, if they were hoping for favours from the Poles they were out of luck. Clearly brimming with pride from their exceptional performances so far in the tournament, Poland were inspired once again and laid siege to the Italian goal, midfielders Kazimierz Deyna and Henryk Kasperczak pulling the strings superbly from deep. Finally, it was Andrzej Szarmach who made use of the opportunity presented to him, heading in Kasperczak's pass for his fifth goal of the tournament. It was two before half-time with Kasperczak again the provider, laying off for the onrushing Deyna to blast into the corner from 25 yards. Poland's assault continued unabated into the second half but they couldn't breach the stubborn Dino Zoff, who pulled off some fine saves. Then,

Stat Attack

Ex-England manager Fabio Capello scored his only World Cup goal against Poland.

with four minutes left, Franco Causio lifted the ball into the area and midfielder Fabio Capello chested the ball down and fired it past Jan Tomaszewski from close range. Italy had four minutes to find the equaliser that would put them through. However, this proved too much as Poland held out for a deserved win to preserve their flawless record, the only one in the tournament, while Italy were left to contemplate first-round failure. Argentina, meanwhile, celebrated joyously back in Munich as the news came through.

First Round results

Group 1

West Germany 1-0 Chile
14/06/74 – West Berlin (Olympiastadion)
West Germany: Maier, Vogts, Schwarzenbeck, Beckenbauer (c), Breitner, Hoeness, Cullmann, Overath (Holzenbein), Grabowski, Muller, Heynckes
Goals: Breitner 18
Chile: Vallejos, Garcia, Quintano, Figueroa, Arias, Rodriguez (Lara), Valdes (c) (Veliz), Reinoso, Caszely, Ahumada, Paez
Sent off: Caszely 67
Referee: Babacan (Turkey)

East Germany 2-0 Australia
14/06/74 – Hamburg (Volksparkstadion)
East Germany: Croy, Bransch (c), Kische, Watzlich, Weise, Pommerenke, Irmscher, Sparwasser, Lowe (Hoffmann), Streich, Vogel
Goals: Curran (og) 58, Streich 72
Australia: Reilly, Utjesenovic, Schafer, Wilson (c), Curran, Richards, Mackay, Rooney, Warren, Alston, Buljevic
Referee: N'Diaye (Senegal)

Australia 0-3 West Germany
18/06/74 – Hamburg (Volksparkstadion)
Australia: Reilly, Utjesenovic, Schafer, Wilson (c), Curran, Richards, Mackay, Rooney, Campbell (Abonyi), Alston, Buljevic (Ollerton)
West Germany: Maier, Vogts, Schwarzenbeck, Beckenbauer (c), Breitner, Hoeness, Cullmann (Wimmer), Overath, Grabowski, Muller, Heynckes (Holzenbein)
Goals: Overath 12, Cullmann 34, Muller 53
Referee: Kamel (Egypt)

Chile 1-1 East Germany
18/06/74 – West Berlin (Olympiastadion)
Chile: Vallejos, Garcia, Quintano, Figueroa, Arias, Socias (Farias), Valdes (c) (Yavar), Reinoso, Veliz, Ahumada, Paez
Goals: Ahumada 69
East Germany: Croy, Bransch (c), Kische, Watzlich, Weise, Seguin (Kreische), Irmscher, Sparwasser, Hoffmann, Streich, Vogel (Ducke)
Goals: Hoffmann 55
Referee: Angonese (Italy)

Australia 0-0 Chile
22/06/74 – West Berlin (Olympiastadion)
Australia: Reilly, Utjesenovic, Schafer, Wilson (c), Curran (Williams), Richards, Mackay, Rooney, Abonyi, Alston (Ollerton), Buljevic
Sent off: Richards 83
Chile: Vallejos, Garcia, Quintano, Figueroa, Arias, Valdes (c) (Farias), Reinoso, Paez, Caszely, Ahumada, Veliz (Yavar)
Referee: Namdar (Iran)

East Germany 1-0 West Germany
22/06/74 – Hamburg (Volksparkstadion)
East Germany: Croy, Bransch (c), Kische, Watzlich, Weise, Kurbjuweit, Irmscher (Hamann), Lauck, Sparwasser, Kreische, Hoffmann
Goals: Sparwasser 77
West Germany: Maier, Vogts, Schwarzenbeck (Hottges), Beckenbauer (c), Breitner, Flohe, Cullmann, Overath (Netzer), Grabowski, Muller, Hoeness
Referee: Barreto (Uruguay)

	Pld	W	D	L	GF	GA	Pts
East Germany	3	2	1	0	4	1	5
West Germany	3	2	0	1	4	1	4
Chile	3	0	2	1	1	2	2
Australia	3	0	1	2	0	5	1

East Germany and West Germany qualified for second round.

Group 2

Brazil 0-0 Yugoslavia
13/06/74 – Frankfurt (Waldstadion)
Brazil: Leao, Nelinho, Luis Pereira, Marinho Peres, Marinho Chagas, Piazza (c), Rivelino, Paulo Cesar, Jairzinho, Valdomiro, Leivinha
Yugoslavia: Maric, Buljan, Katalinski, Bogicevic, Hadziabdic, Muzinic, Oblak, Acimovic, Petkovic, Surjak, Dzajic (c)
Referee: Scheurer (Switzerland)

Zaire 0-2 Scotland
14/06/74 – Dortmund (Westfalenstadion)
Zaire: Kazadi, Mwepu, Mukombo, Bwanga, Lobilo, Kilasu, Maku (Kembo), Mana, Ndaye, Kidumu (c) (Kibonge), Kakoko
Scotland: Harvey, Jardine, Holton, Blackley, McGrain, Bremner (c), Hay, Lorimer, Dalglish (Hutchison), Jordan, Law
Goals: Lorimer 26, Jordan 34
Referee: Schulenburg (West Germany)

Scotland 0-0 Brazil
18/06/74 – Frankfurt (Waldstadion)
Scotland: Harvey, Jardine, Holton, Buchan, McGrain, Bremner (c), Hay, Lorimer, Dalglish, Jordan, Morgan
Brazil: Leao, Nelinho, Luis Pereira, Marinho Peres, Marinho Chagas, Piazza (c), Rivelino, Paulo Cesar, Jairzinho, Mirandinha, Leivinha (Carpegiani)
Referee: Van Gemert (Holland)

Yugoslavia 9-0 Zaire
18/06/74 – Gelsenkirchen (Parkstadion)
Yugoslavia: Maric, Buljan, Katalinski, Bogicevic, Hadziabdic, Petkovic, Oblak, Acimovic, Bajevic, Surjak, Dzajic (c)
Goals: Bajevic 8, 30, 81, Dzajic 14, Surjak 18, Katalinski 22, Bogicevic 35, Oblak 61, Petkovic 65
Zaire: Kazadi (Tubilandu), Mwepu, Mukombo, Bwanga, Lobilo, Kilasu, Kembo, Mana, Ndaye, Kidumu (c), Kakoko (Maku)
Sent off: Ndaye 22
Referee: Delgado (Colombia)

Scotland 1-1 Yugoslavia
22/06/74 – Frankfurt (Waldstadion)
Scotland: Harvey, Jardine, Holton, Buchan, McGrain, Bremner (c), Hay, Lorimer, Dalglish (Hutchison), Jordan, Morgan
Goals: Jordan 88
Yugoslavia: Maric, Buljan, Katalinski, Bogicevic, Hadziabdic, Petkovic, Oblak, Acimovic, Bajevic (Karasi), Surjak, Dzajic (c)
Goals: Karasi 81
Referee: Archundia (Mexico)

Zaire 0-3 Brazil
22/06/74 – Gelsenkirchen (Parkstadion)
Zaire: Kazadi, Mwepu, Mukombo, Bwanga, Lobilo, Kibonge, Tshinabu (Kembo), Mana, Ntumba, Kidumu (c) (Kilasu), Maku
Brazil: Leao, Nelinho, Luis Pereira, Marinho Peres, Marinho Chagas, Piazza (c) (Mirandinha), Rivelino, Carpegiani, Jairzinho, Leivinha (Valdomiro), Edu
Goals: Jairzinho 12, Rivelino 66, Valdomiro 79
Referee: Rainea (Romania)

	Pld	W	D	L	GF	GA	Pts
Yugoslavia	3	1	2	0	10	1	4
Brazil	3	1	2	0	3	0	4
Scotland	3	1	2	0	3	1	4
Zaire	3	0	0	3	0	14	0

Yugoslavia and Brazil qualified for second round.

Group 3

Uruguay 0-2 Holland
15/06/74 – Hanover (Niedersachsenstadion)
Uruguay: Mazurkiewicz, Forlan, Jauregui, Masnik (c), Pavoni, Esparrago, Montero Castillo, Rocha, Cubilla (Milar), Morena, Mantegazza
Sent off: Montero Castillo 69
Holland: Jongbloed, Suurbier, Rijsbergen, Haan, Krol, Jansen, Neeskens, Van Hanegem, Rep, Cruyff (c), Rensenbrink
Goals: Rep 16, 86
Referee: Palotai (Hungary)

Sweden 0-0 Bulgaria
15/06/74 – Dusseldorf (Rheinstadion)
Sweden: Hellstrom, Olsson, Andersson, Karlsson, B Larsson (c), Grahn, Tapper, Kindvall (Magnusson), Torstensson, Sandberg, Edstrom
Bulgaria: Goranov, T Vasilev, Ivkov, Penev, Velichkov, Kolev, Bonev (c), Nikodimov, Voinov (Mihailov), Panov (M Vasilev), Denev
Referee: Perez Nunez (Peru)

Bulgaria 1-1 Uruguay
19/06/74 – Hanover (Niedersachsenstadion)
Bulgaria: Goranov, T Vasilev, Ivkov, Penev, Velichkov, Kolev, Bonev (c), Nikodimov (Mihailov), Voinov, Panov, Denev
Goals: Bonev 75
Uruguay: Mazurkiewicz (c), Forlan, Jauregui, Garisto (Masnik), Pavoni, Esparrago, Rocha, Mantegazza (Cardaccio), Milar, Morena, Corbo
Goals: Pavoni 87
Referee: Taylor (England)

Holland 0-0 Sweden
19/06/74 – Dortmund (Westfalenstadion)
Holland: Jongbloed, Suurbier, Rijsbergen, Haan, Krol, Jansen, Neeskens, Van Hanegem (De Jong), Rep, Cruyff (c), Keizer
Sweden: Hellstrom, Olsson (Grip), Andersson, Nordqvist (c), Karlsson, B Larsson, Grahn, Tapper (Persson), Ejderstedt, Sandberg, Edstrom
Referee: Winsemann (Canada)

Bulgaria 1-4 Holland
23/06/74 – Dortmund (Westfalenstadion)
Bulgaria: Staikov, T Vasilev, Ivkov, Penev, Velichkov, Kolev, Bonev (c), Stoyanov (Mihailov), Voinov, Panov (Borisov), Denev
Goals: Krol (og) 78
Holland: Jongbloed, Suurbier, Rijsbergen, Haan, Krol, Jansen, Neeskens (De Jong), Van Hanegem (Israel), Rep, Cruyff (c), Rensenbrink
Goals: Neeskens pen 5, pen 45, Rep 71, De Jong 88
Referee: Boskovic (Australia)

Sweden 3-0 Uruguay
23/06/74 – Dusseldorf (Rheinstadion)
Sweden: Hellstrom, Grip, Andersson, Nordqvist (c), Karlsson, B Larsson, Grahn, Magnusson (Ahlstrom), Kindvall (Torstensson), Sandberg, Edstrom
Goals: Edstrom 46, 77, Sandberg 74
Uruguay: Mazurkiewicz (c), Forlan, Jauregui, Garisto (Masnik), Pavoni, Esparrago, Rocha, Mantegazza, Milar, Morena, Corbo (Cubilla)
Referee: Linemayr (Austria)

	Pld	W	D	L	GF	GA	Pts
Holland	3	2	1	0	6	1	5
Sweden	3	1	2	0	3	0	4
Bulgaria	3	0	2	1	2	5	2
Uruguay	3	0	1	2	1	6	1

Holland and Sweden qualified for second round.

Group 4

Italy 3-1 Haiti
15/06/74 – Munich (Olympiastadion)
Italy: Zoff, Spinosi, Morini, Burgnich, Facchetti (c), Mazzola, Capello, Rivera, Benetti, Chinaglia (Anastasi), Riva
Goals: Rivera 52, Benetti 66, Anastasi 79
Haiti: Francillon, Bayonne, Jean-Joseph, Nazaire (c), Auguste, Antoine, Desir, Vorbe, Francois, G Saint-Vil (Barthelemy), Sanon
Goals: Sanon 46
Referee: Llobregat (Venezuela)

Poland 3-2 Argentina
15/06/74 – Stuttgart (Neckarstadion)
Poland: Tomaszewski, Szymanowski, Gorgon, Zmuda, Musial, Kasperczak, Deyna (c), Maszczyk, Lato, Szarmach (Domarski), Gadocha (Cmikiewicz)
Goals: Lato 7, 62, Szarmach 8
Argentina: Carnevali, Bargas (Telch), Wolff, Perfumo (c), Heredia, Sa, Brindisi (Houseman), Babington, Balbuena, Ayala, Kempes
Goals: Heredia 60, Babington 66
Referee: Thomas (Wales)

Argentina 1-1 Italy
19/06/74 – Stuttgart (Neckarstadion)
Argentina: Carnevali, Wolff (Glaria), Perfumo (c), Heredia, Sa, Telch, Babington, Houseman, Yazalde (Chazarreta), Ayala, Kempes
Goals: Houseman 19
Italy: Zoff, Spinosi, Morini (Wilson), Burgnich, Facchetti (c), Mazzola, Capello, Rivera (Causio), Benetti, Anastasi, Riva
Goals: Perfumo (og) 35
Referee: Kazakov (USSR)

Haiti 0-7 Poland
19/06/74 – Munich (Olympiastadion)
Haiti: Francillon, Bayonne, Andre (Barthelemy), Nazaire (c), Auguste, Antoine, Desir, Vorbe, Francois, Sanon, R Saint-Vil (Racine)
Poland: Tomaszewski, Szymanowski, Gorgon, Zmuda, Musial (Gut), Kasperczak, Deyna (c), Maszczyk (Cmikiewicz), Lato, Szarmach, Gadocha
Goals: Lato 17, 87, Deyna 18, Szarmach 30, 34, 50, Gorgon 31
Referee: Suppiah (Singapore)

Argentina 4-1 Haiti
23/06/74 – Munich (Olympiastadion)
Argentina: Carnevali, Wolff, Perfumo (c), Heredia, Sa, Telch, Babington, Houseman (Brindisi), Yazalde, Ayala, Kempes (Balbuena)
Goals: Yazalde 15, 68, Houseman 18, Ayala 55
Haiti: Francillon, Bayonne, Ducoste, Nazaire (c) (JM Leandre), Louis, Antoine, Desir, Vorbe, Racine, G Saint-Vil (F Leandre), Sanon
Goals: Sanon 63
Referee: Sanchez Ibanez (Spain)

Poland 2-1 Italy
23/06/74 – Stuttgart (Neckarstadion)
Poland: Tomaszewski, Szymanowski, Gorgon, Zmuda, Musial, Kasperczak, Deyna (c), Maszczyk, Lato, Szarmach (Cmikiewicz), Gadocha
Goals: Szarmach 38, Deyna 44
Italy: Zoff, Spinosi, Morini, Burgnich (Wilson), Facchetti (c), Mazzola, Capello, Causio, Benetti, Chinaglia (Boninsegna), Anastasi
Goals: Capello 86
Referee: Weyland (West Germany)

	Pld	W	D	L	GF	GA	Pts
Poland	3	3	0	0	12	3	6
Argentina	3	1	1	1	7	5	3
Italy	3	1	1	1	5	4	3
Haiti	3	0	0	3	2	14	0

Poland and Argentina qualified for second round.

World Cup Great – Gianni Rivera (Italy)

Despite being one of the most gifted Italian players of all time, playmaker Gianni Rivera was often used only sparingly by the Italian national team. Maybe this was because Rivera's game revolved around being the hub of the team, the same role Sandro Mazzola preferred. However, not even the highly talented Mazzola could hold a candle to Rivera at top form.

Rivera came up through the youth ranks of local club Alessandria, making his senior debut when he was just 15 in 1959. Only a year later, he was snapped up by top club AC Milan, who saw him as an ideal replacement for their ageing Uruguayan star Juan Schiaffino. Despite being only 16 at the time, he quickly forced himself into the club's first team plans, being a key part of the title winning side of 1962. That summer, the 18-year-old travelled to his first World Cup. There he won his first cap in a 0-0 draw with West Germany. However, Italy's poor performance in the tournament, exiting in the first round, soon resulted in Rivera becoming a mainstay of the national side as well as at club level.

On his return to Milan, the teenage Rivera was on top form and was the major inspiration behind Milan becoming the first Italian side to win the European Cup, beating holders Benfica in the final in 1963. Rivera dictated the play brilliantly throughout the season and his form was so good that the youngster finished runner-up in the voting for the European Footballer of the Year. Come 1966, Rivera got a second shot at a World Cup, this time as a key player. However, the tournament did not transpire as he might have hoped as Italy lost shockingly to North Korea and went out straight away. On their return to Italy, Rivera and his team mates were pelted with tomatoes!

In 1968, however, the Italian national team was to go through a revival which culminated in winning the European Championship that year. Rivera was a key part of the team but sadly was forced out of the final due to injury. However, he would have another moment of glory the following year, guiding Milan to their second European Cup victory and this time carrying off the European Footballer of the Year award as well.

However, despite being the Ballon d'Or holder, Rivera was not considered a first-team regular by Italy coach Ferruccio Valcareggi, who believed he and Mazzola could not play together and surprisingly started the Inter playmaker ahead of him. However, after an impressive cameo appearance from the bench in Italy's final group game of the 1970 World Cup, Valcareggi took to playing the two for 45 minutes each, Mazzola in the first half and Rivera in the second. This tactic brought victory over Mexico and West Germany to carry the Azzurri into the final, though notably in both games Italy improved enormously once the slick Rivera took to the field. The Milan star scored twice en route to the final, including the crucial extra-time winner against the Germans. However, in the final he was left on the bench until the dying moments, arriving far too late to turn around the 4-1 defeat.

Rivera's last World Cup appearance came at the age of 30 in 1974. Rivera played the first two games and was the driving force behind a win and a draw in a solid start. However, Valcareggi strangely left him out of the crunch match with Poland. Without their star player, Italy lost 2-1 and were out of the tournament. Rivera would never play for Italy again, leaving with 60 caps and 14 goals. Rivera continued to play for Milan until 1979, fittingly retiring by winning the title in his last season.

That Rivera didn't make more appearances for Italy is probably a large reason why the national team underperformed for so much of the 1960s and 70s. Various coaches appeared reluctant to build a team around him, despite Milan illustrating how effective he was when given control. Surely Rivera's brilliant performances for Italy when he was on the field were enough to prove his worth. Blessed with outstanding touch and vision, Rivera was a supremely able playmaker and maybe had he been the key component of the 1970 team instead of just a substitute then the Azzurri might have stood more of a chance against Brazil in the final.

Second Round Group Draw

Group A

East Germany (Winner Group One)
Brazil (Runner-up Group Two)
Holland (Winner Group Three)
Argentina (Runner-up Group Four)

Group B

West Germany (Runner-up Group One)
Yugoslavia (Winner Group Two)
Sweden (Runner-up Group Three)
Poland (Winner Group Four)

Second Round – First series

The second round seemed to have thrown up two rather uneven groups. Group A featured favourites Holland, holders Brazil and a fine Argentina side as well as the unfortunate East Germans, who would not have had anything like as tough a draw had they not beaten the hosts West Germany, who seemed, meanwhile, to have a relatively simple passage out of Group B. Poland had looked impressive but Yugoslavia and Sweden would hardly fill the hosts with fear in the same way as Brazil and Holland might have. The round-robin format of the first round groups would remain here, with the winners facing one another in the final and the runners-up meeting in the third-place play-off.

In Group B, **West Germany** got off to the perfect start with a simple victory over **Yugoslavia**. The Germans fielded a much-changed line-up after their shock loss to their eastern neighbours but the new men for the most part seemed to settle in with no problems and the hosts dominated the game from start to finish. Paul Breitner put them ahead in typical fashion five minutes before half-time, collecting the ball 30 yards from goal, stepping past a defender and hammering his shot into the top corner. The Yugoslavs seemed to show surprisingly little ambition to get themselves back into the game and with eight minutes remaining the Germans confirmed victory with a second goal, substitute Uli Hoeness bursting down the right flank and pulling back for Gerd Muller to fire in his second of the tournament.

In Stuttgart, where they had already had so much success, **Poland** looked to open with victory over **Sweden**, who had largely failed to impress so far. Predictably it was the Poles who took the lead just before the break, Andrzej Szarmach's knockdown at the far post allowing Grzegorz Lato to head the ball in from a yard out for the winger's fifth goal of the tournament. However, the Poles failed to maintain their level of dominance in the second period and for the first time in the competition were forced to hold onto their lead as they came under attack. Just past the hour, Conny Torstensson burst into the box and was tripped by Jerzy Gorgon. Staffan Tapper had the chance to equalise from the spot but the inspired Jan Tomaszewski threw himself to his right to brilliantly tip the spot-kick round the post. Galvanised by Tomaszewski's heroics, Poland held on for a crucial win.

In Group A, **East Germany** straight away faced the formidable task of getting something from their clash with reigning champions **Brazil** in Hanover. Putting their onus on defence, the Germans heroically held out for an hour, resisting waves of Brazilian attacks. It would take something special to breach Jurgen Croy and his defence and that was what Rivelino finally produced, smashing a pinpoint free-kick through the tiniest of gaps in the defensive wall to confirm Brazil's narrow 1-0 victory. East Germany had been far from disgraced but they now faced an upward struggle if they were to be in with a hope of reaching the final.

Holland swaggered into Gelsenkirchen and gave an instant demonstration of their title credentials, sweeping away **Argentina** by an emphatic score of 4-0. Just ten minutes in, Wim Van Hanegem's lofted pass into the area picked out the run of Johan Cruyff and the Barcelona maestro pulled the ball down in breathtaking fashion, rounded the flailing Daniel Carnevali and tucked the ball in. Holland's movement and passing were sublime and altogether too much for the outclassed South Americans. One phenomenal team move saw Van Hanegem and Rob Rensenbrink combine to set up the excellent Johan Neeskens but his powerful drive was ruled out for a marginal offside. Nevertheless, Holland were two goals to the good minutes later. Neeskens sent in a corner, Carnevali punched it out but left-back Ruud Krol drove in a thunderous first-time shot from the edge of the area which flew into the back of the net. In the second half a storm lashed the stadium and the driving rain was not at all conducive to free-flowing football. Still, this didn't stop the Dutch and they would score twice more before the end. First, Cruyff's perfect cross from the left was headed in at the far post by Johnny Rep before at the death Van Hanegem played a slick one-two with Wim Jansen, burst into the area and though Carnevali blocked off his shot, Cruyff was running in to slide in the follow-up from an acute angle. Holland had obliterated Argentina's challenge and laid down a formidable marker to the rest.

> ## Only at the World Cup
>
> Rivelino's free-kick winner against East Germany was fabulously executed. Jairzinho, loitering in the wall, ducked at the crucial moment, Rivelino's effort flying through the tiny gap and leaving keeper Croy with no chance.

Second Round – Second series

South American giants **Brazil** and **Argentina** faced each other in Hanover, the Argentineans desperate for victory coming off the back of the footballing lesson the Dutch had taught them four days earlier. This Brazilian side placed defence above attack but some of the individual players were still blessed with sublime skill and a glorious one-touch team move set up the first goal just past the half-hour, the ball eventually worked for Rivelino to blast into the corner from 25 yards. However, three minutes later their great rivals were level.

Winning a free-kick on the edge of the box, Miguel Brindisi thumped home a swerving shot off the underside of the bar, though keeper Emerson Leao, who was in the perfect position, really should have saved it. In the end, however, it wasn't to matter as Jairzinho provided the champions with a second-half winner, Ze Maria crossing from the right and the winger arriving to head in.

Holland maintained their seemingly inevitable march to the final by ending **East Germany**'s challenge. With the game just minutes old, a goalmouth scramble saw the ball fly around the Germans' area before Johan Neeskens eventually slid it in in style. To their credit, East Germany did go on the attack in a vain attempt to stay in the tournament but the Dutch proved altogether too strong. Victory was confirmed when Johnny Rep went on a slaloming run before squaring for the dangerous Rob Rensenbrink to fire in his first goal of the tournament.

Back in Group B, **Poland** took on **Yugoslavia** in Frankfurt. The Poles continued to surprise and impress at the tournament and were by far the better team from the off. The usually reliable Andrzej Szarmach uncharacteristically blazed over the bar with the goal gaping but minutes later the Poles won a penalty for an off-the-ball infringement immediately following a free-kick. Captain Kazimierz Deyna stepped up and coolly sent keeper Maric the wrong way for 1-0. However, completely against the run of play, the Slavs equalised just before half-time, Jurica Jerkovic playing an exquisite through-ball for Stanislav Karasi and the striker deceived Tomaszewski with a quick body feint before firing into the back of the net. Still, the Poles were to get the winner they so richly deserved in the second half, little Grzegorz Lato running in to head in Gadocha's corner at the near post. They had maintained their 100% record in the tournament and still had every chance of reaching the final.

In the pouring rain at Dusseldorf, **West Germany** too got a crucial win over **Sweden**, though here the Scandinavians finally found their form to run the Germans exceptionally close in a thrilling contest. After Gerd Muller was uncharacteristically wasteful in front of goal, the first goal, to the crowd's shock, went to the Swedes, striker Ralf Edstrom lurking on the edge of the area and pouncing when the German defence only partially cleared a Swedish attack, lashing in a perfect left-foot volley past a stunned Sepp Maier. In the second half, the Germans began to find their form and soon after the break they took the lead with a quick-fire double salvo. First, Uli Hoeness' run found Muller and the striker laid off for Wolfgang Overath to fire into the corner. Seconds later, another Muller lay-off allowed Rainer Bonhof to let fly from the edge of the area and though Ronnie Hellstrom did brilliantly to tip the shot onto the post, it trickled over the line. However, the Swedes were not deterred and they hit back with a goal less than a minute later. The German defence did not properly deal with a long cross from the right and Roland Sandberg was lurking to slide the ball in at the far post. Germany coach Helmut Schon, knowing it was crucial his team won to keep pace with Poland, threw on the dangerous Jurgen Grabowski from the bench and the move proved decisive. Within minutes, Muller received the ball in the area and though he himself was closed off, he found Bernd Holzenbein who in turn worked the ball to Grabowski and the winger fired home. Any hopes of a Swedish comeback were ended two minutes from time when Muller was felled in the area, the exceptional Hoeness taking the responsibility for the spot-kick and scoring with ease. Going into the final games, the Germans were in the driving seat.

Second Round – Third series

In Frankfurt, **West Germany** and **Poland** faced one another for a place in the final. The match had to be delayed by half an hour after the terrible weather that had persisted throughout the tournament saw a downpour of almost biblical proportions and some of the water had to be removed from the pitch. The Germans knew that a draw would be enough to see them through to the final and so they sat back, knowing the Poles would be forced to come at them, leaving themselves open at the back. Despite the Poles

Only at the World Cup

The terrible weather throughout the tournament culminated in a delayed start to the Poland-West Germany game because of the amount of water on the pitch after a huge rainstorm.

going close early on, the hosts' tactics bore fruit when they won a second-half penalty. However, Jan Tomaszewski was again the Polish hero, keeping out Uli Hoeness' effort to preserve parity. Nevertheless, it was the Germans who scored the game's only goal, the ever-dangerous Gerd Muller finding the space in the area to beat the heroic Tomaszewski, notching his 13th career World Cup goal, taking him level with Just Fontaine at the top of the all-time scoring charts. Poland had performed brilliantly throughout the tournament but they had come up just short. It would be the hosts who would compete in the final.

Stat Attack

Jan Tomaszewski became the first keeper to save two penalties in a single World Cup.

Meanwhile, **Sweden** and **Yugoslavia** contested a meaningless game, since both teams had already been eliminated. Ivica Surjak put the Eastern Europeans ahead from Dragan Dzajic's cross but within minutes Ralf Edstrom had blasted in his fourth goal of the tournament to equalise. Deservedly, it was the Scandinavians, by far the more willing side, who snatched a winner five minutes from the end, Conny Torstensson beating Maric in the Yugoslavian goal to end their tournament on a high.

Another game with nothing but pride at stake took place at Gelsenkirchen, where **Argentina** and **East Germany** faced one another, both assured of departing after the match. The Argentineans were generally favoured but it was their opponents who took the lead, the dangerous Joachim Streich popping up to head them into a surprise lead. Nevertheless, the South Americans steeled themselves and hit back, Mario Kempes setting up the exceptional Rene Houseman to score his third goal of the tournament. There would be no winner for either side, however, and both would have to settle with just a point to satisfy them on their journeys home.

At Dortmund, **Holland** faced **Brazil** in a potentially mouth-watering game, with a place in the final at stake. Sadly, the match was far from the spectacle expected. The Dutch, playing a similar style of football to the great Brazilian team of four years earlier, were far too good for the holders, who again resorted to brutal tactics and negativity, pulling everyone behind the ball and stopping their opponents with sly fouls. Holland were not impressed but allowed themselves to be dragged into the physicality the Brazilians were exhibiting, committing plenty of fouls themselves rather than just getting on with their game. In the second period, however, the Dutch returned to their glorious "Total Football" and the Brazilians had no answer. Johan Neeskens burst clear down the middle, fed Cruyff on the right flank and ran into the box to meet his captain's cross with a cheeky finish, flicking the ball over the head of the helpless Leao. 15 minutes later and the game was over, slick passing down the left flank releasing Ruud Krol and the full-back's cross was converted in style by Cruyff, who met it with a crisp aerial volley. Brazil, needing to win to have any hope of retaining their title, resorted to petulance and violence. Centre-back Luis Pereira savagely scythed down his tormentor Neeskens and received a red card for his troubles. Brazil had greatly damaged their own reputation and been beaten by a team far more talented and more willing to attack than themselves. Holland were most certainly well deserving of their first ever place in a World Cup final.

Second Round results

Group A

Brazil 1-0 East Germany
26/06/74 – Hanover (Niedersachsenstadion)
Brazil: Leao, Ze Maria, Luis Pereira, Marinho Peres (c), Marinho Chagas, Carpegiani, Dirceu, Rivelino, Jairzinho, Valdomiro, Paulo Cesar
Goals: Rivelino 60
East Germany: Croy, Bransch (c), Kische, Watzlich, Weise, Kurbjuweit, Hamann (Irmscher), Lauck (Lowe), Sparwasser, Hoffmann, Streich
Referee: Thomas (Wales)

Holland 4-0 Argentina
26/06/74 – Gelsenkirchen (Parkstadion)
Holland: Jongbloed, Suurbier (Israel), Rijsbergen, Haan, Krol, Jansen, Neeskens, Van Hanegem, Rep, Cruyff (c), Rensenbrink
Goals: Cruyff 10, 90, Krol 25, Rep 73
Argentina: Carnevali, Wolff (Glaria), Perfumo (c), Heredia, Sa, Telch, Squeo, Houseman (Kempes), Yazalde, Ayala, Balbuena
Referee: Davidson (Scotland)

Argentina 1-2 Brazil
30/06/74 – Hanover (Niedersachsenstadion)
Argentina: Carnevali, Bargas, Heredia, Sa (Carrascosa), Glaria, Squeo, Brindisi (c), Babington, Balbuena, Ayala, Kempes (Houseman)
Goals: Brindisi 35
Brazil: Leao, Ze Maria, Luis Pereira, Marinho Peres (c), Marinho Chagas, Carpegiani, Dirceu, Rivelino, Jairzinho, Valdomiro, Paulo Cesar
Goals: Rivelino 32, Jairzinho 49
Referee: Loraux (Belgium)

East Germany 0-2 Holland
30/06/74 – Gelsenkirchen (Parkstadion)
East Germany: Croy, Kurbjuweit, Bransch (c), Kische, Weise, Pommerenke, Schnuphase, Lauck (Kreische), Sparwasser, Lowe (Ducke), Hoffmann
Holland: Jongbloed, Suurbier, Rijsbergen, Haan, Krol, Jansen, Neeskens, Van Hanegem, Rep, Cruyff (c), Rensenbrink
Goals: Neeskens 13, Rensenbrink 59
Referee: Scheurer (Switzerland)

Argentina 1-1 East Germany
03/07/74 – Gelsenkirchen (Parkstadion)
Argentina: Fillol, Bargas, Wolff (c), Heredia, Carrascosa, Telch, Brindisi, Babington, Houseman, Ayala, Kempes
Goals: Houseman 20
East Germany: Croy, Kurbjuweit, Bransch (c), Kische, Weise, Pommerenke, Schnuphase, Sparwasser, Lowe (Vogel), Streich (Ducke), Hoffmann
Goals: Streich 14
Referee: Taylor (England)

Holland 2-0 Brazil
03/07/74 – Dortmund (Westfalenstadion)
Holland: Jongbloed, Suurbier, Rijsbergen, Haan, Krol, Jansen, Neeskens (Israel), Van Hanegem, Rep, Cruyff (c), Rensenbrink (De Jong)
Goals: Neeskens 50, Cruyff 65
Brazil: Leao, Ze Maria, Luis Pereira, Marinho Peres (c), Marinho Chagas, Carpegiani, Dirceu, Rivelino, Jairzinho, Valdomiro, Paulo Cesar (Mirandinha)
Sent off: Luis Pereira 84
Referee: Tschenscher (West Germany)

	Pld	W	D	L	GF	GA	Pts
Holland	3	3	0	0	8	0	6
Brazil	3	2	0	1	3	3	4
East Germany	3	0	1	2	1	4	1
Argentina	3	0	1	2	2	7	1

Holland qualified for final, Brazil to third-place play-off.

Group B

Yugoslavia 0-2 West Germany
26/06/74 – Dusseldorf (Rheinstadion)
Yugoslavia: Maric, Buljan, Katalinski, Muzinic, Hadziabdic, Popivoda, Oblak (Jerkovic), Acimovic, Surjak, Karasi, Dzajic (c) (Petkovic)
West Germany: Maier, Vogts, Schwarzenbeck, Beckenbauer (c), Breitner, Wimmer (Hoeness), Bonhof, Overath, Herzog, Muller, Holzenbein (Flohe)
Goals: Breitner 39, Muller 82
Referee: Marques (Brazil)

Sweden 0-1 Poland
26/06/74 – Stuttgart (Neckarstadion)
Sweden: Hellstrom, Grip, Andersson (Augustsson), Nordqvist (c), Karlsson, B Larsson, Grahn, Tapper (Ahlstrom), Torstensson, Sandberg, Edstrom
Poland: Tomaszewski, Szymanowski, Gorgon, Zmuda, Gut, Kasperczak, Deyna (c), Maszczyk, Lato, Szarmach (Kmiecik), Gadocha
Goals: Lato 43
Referee: Barreto (Uruguay)

Poland 2-1 Yugoslavia

30/06/74 – Frankfurt (Waldstadion)

Poland: Tomaszewski, Szymanowski, Gorgon, Zmuda, Musial, Kasperczak, Deyna (c) (Domarski), Maszczyk, Lato, Szarmach (Cmikiewicz), Gadocha

Goals: Deyna pen 24, Lato 62

Yugoslavia: Maric, Buljan, Katalinski, Bogicevic, Hadziabdic, Petkovic (V Petrovic), Oblak (Jerkovic), Acimovic (c), Bajevic, Karasi, Surjak

Goals: Karasi 43

Referee: Glockner (East Germany)

West Germany 4-2 Sweden

30/06/74 – Dusseldorf (Rheinstadion)

West Germany: Maier, Vogts, Schwarzenbeck, Beckenbauer (c), Breitner, Hoeness, Bonhof, Overath, Herzog (Grabowski), Muller, Holzenbein (Flohe)

Goals: Overath 51, Bonhof 52, Grabowski 76, Hoeness pen 89

Sweden: Hellstrom, Olsson, Nordqvist (c), Augustsson, Karlsson, B Larsson (Ejderstedt), Grahn, Tapper, Torstensson, Sandberg, Edstrom

Goals: Edstrom 24, Sandberg 53

Referee: Kazakov (USSR)

Poland 0-1 West Germany

03/07/74 – Frankfurt (Waldstadion)

Poland: Tomaszewski, Szymanowski, Gorgon, Zmuda, Musial, Kasperczak (Cmikiewicz), Deyna (c), Maszczyk (Kmiecik), Lato, Domarski, Gadocha

West Germany: Maier, Vogts, Schwarzenbeck, Beckenbauer (c), Breitner, Hoeness, Bonhof, Overath, Grabowski, Muller, Holzenbein

Goals: Muller 76

Referee: Linemayr (Austria)

Sweden 2-1 Yugoslavia

03/07/74 – Dusseldorf (Rheinstadion)

Sweden: Hellstrom, Olsson, Nordqvist (c), Augustsson, Karlsson, Tapper, Grahn, Persson, Torstensson, Sandberg, Edstrom

Goals: Edstrom 29, Torstensson 85

Yugoslavia: Maric, Buljan, Katalinski, Bogicevic, Hadziabdic, Pavlovic (Peruzovic), Jerkovic, Acimovic, V Petrovic (Karasi), Surjak, Dzajic (c)

Goals: Surjak 27

Referee: Pestarino (Argentina)

	Pld	W	D	L	GF	GA	Pts
West Germany	3	3	0	0	7	2	6
Poland	3	2	0	1	3	2	4
Sweden	3	1	0	2	4	6	2
Yugoslavia	3	0	0	3	2	6	0

West Germany qualified for final, Poland to third-place play-off.

Third-place Play-off

In Munich, **Brazil** and **Poland** played off for the right to call themselves the world's third best team. Both sides kept the core of their first-choice line-up but unsurprisingly it was the Poles, who had never been anywhere near this far before, who were the hungrier; the Brazilians, for whom not finishing first was failure, seemed largely disinterested. As it happened, however, even the Brazilians playing at their best may well have struggled against this fine Polish side. Though the South Americans struck the post from close range, Poland took a deserved lead when midfielder Zygmunt Maszczyk found Grzegorz Lato and the little winger burst down the right flank, leaving Marinho Peres for dead before slotting the ball expertly into the far corner for a fabulous solo goal. The Poles should have won by more, Kazimierz Deyna twice sending Lato clear again with exquisite through-balls but Emerson Leao denying him on both occasions. Nevertheless, Lato's goal, his seventh in the tournament, saw him finish as top scorer and his nation claim the bronze medal, an achievement beyond their wildest dreams but one which they richly deserved.

Third-place Play-off result

Brazil 0-1 Poland
06/07/74 – Munich (Olympiastadion)
Brazil: Leao, Ze Maria, Alfredo, Marinho Peres (c), Marinho Chagas, Carpegiani, Dirceu, Rivelino, Jairzinho, Valdomiro, Ademir (Mirandinha)
Poland: Tomaszewski, Szymanowski, Gorgon, Zmuda, Musial, Kasperczak (Cmikiewicz), Deyna (c), Maszczyk, Lato, Szarmach (Kapka), Gadocha
Goals: Lato 76
Referee: Angonese (Italy)

Poland claimed third place.

World Cup Great – Jairzinho (Brazil)

Although Garrincha is almost universally regarded as Brazil's greatest ever right winger, his successor for the national team, Jairzinho, lost very little in comparison with his legendary predecessor. A more conventional player than the maverick Garrincha, Jairzinho's game was based around his devastating combination of pace and strength, which he used to terrify defences for years.

Jairzinho first emerged through the youth ranks of his local Rio club Botafogo as a teenager in the early 1960s. At the time, Garrincha was the star man for club and country, turning in inspired performances on the right wing. The youngster idolised the established star and soon got his wish to play alongside his hero. However, Garrincha's presence meant the young winger had to play on his less favoured left flank or as a striker. Still, he performed admirably in these positions, despite being a natural right winger, and impressed enough to win his first cap for Brazil in 1964 at the age of 19.

Two years later, Jairzinho was one of a crop of untested youngsters taken to the 1966 World Cup. Unlike most of them, Jairzinho was one of the few to be given a starting place from the outset, playing in a team of veterans. Again, however, the presence of Garrincha forced him to ply his trade on the left wing. Despite some flashes of skill, hinting at his ability, Jairzinho was unable to find his best form in this unfamiliar position and with a misfiring team around him, he and Brazil exited the tournament in the first round.

Garrincha called time on his national career after the tournament and Jairzinho effortlessly took over his position on the right wing, both for Botafogo and Brazil. By the time of the 1970 World Cup, Jairzinho was 25 and one of the stars of the Brazil team. Playing on the right of a front three that was built around the great Pelé, Jairzinho proved a perfect foil to the creative promptings of his team mates. The likes of Pelé, Tostao, Gerson and Rivelino all were possessed of supreme passing ability and were able to dictate the play. The speed and strength of Jairzinho, meanwhile, made him the perfect player to feed off his team mates' play, his running tormenting opponents. With so much creative ammunition around him, Jairzinho was unsurprisingly one of the players of the tournament, matching Gyorgy Sarosi, Alcides Ghiggia and Just Fontaine before him by scoring in every game of the tournament, scoring two in the first match against Czechoslovakia and one in each match after that, including in the 4-1 victory over Italy in the final, for a total of seven goals in six games, making him the tournament's second highest scorer. Some of his goals featured superb individual runs and dribbles, highlighting his phenomenal ability.

Jairzinho's third bite of the World Cup cherry came in Germany in 1974. Brazil were a much changed side and only he and Rivelino remained of the legendary five gunslingers of 1970. With the emphasis now firmly on defence, Brazil and Jairzinho were given far less licence to thrill but the winger did at least get himself on the scoresheet twice, giving him a total of nine career World Cup goals. Jairzinho would play on for Brazil until March 1982, though he was left out of the 1978 World Cup squad, denying him the chance of a fourth tournament.

The winger left Botafogo in 1974 and would live a nomadic existence in his later footballing years. After a brief spell at Marseille, he soon returned to Brazil and won the Libertadores Cup with Cruzeiro in 1976. He went through several other South American clubs before eventually retiring aged 37 in 1982.

Jairzinho's name will forever be associated with his exploits in the 1970 World Cup but this was merely the highlight of a long and successful career. His pace, trickery and strength on the right wing made him far too hot for most defenders to handle and with the promptings of talented team mates around him, he was all but unstoppable. That Brazil missed the great Garrincha as little as they did in the 1970s is testament to Jairzinho's brilliance.

World Cup Final

The tenth World Cup final was the one that the organisers had hoped it would be: the favourites **Holland**, full of dash, skill and invention, masterminded by their untouchable captain Johan Cruyff; and the hosts and reigning European champions **West Germany**, solid, determined and well-organised, led from the back by the composed and unflappable Franz Beckenbauer. Most expected the Dutch to win; indeed, many thought it would be a travesty if their brilliant team who had so lit up the tournament did not carry off the trophy. Nevertheless, the Germans were a fine all-round footballing side and with the added bonus of a passionate home crowd at Munich's Olympiastadion they were a force to be reckoned with. The Dutch kicked off and there was instant sensation. In trademark fashion, Holland worked a series of accurate short passes between team mates, leaving the Germans chasing shadows, before Cruyff decided to up the tempo, receiving the ball on the halfway line, dropping his shoulder and bursting past his marker Berti Vogts. Cruyff sprinted into the area and attacking midfielder Uli Hoeness, tracking back, brought him down with a trip. English referee Jack Taylor had no hesitation in pointing to the spot for a clear penalty, the first in a final. Johan Neeskens stepped up and smashed the ball straight down the middle. 1-0 and the first German player to touch the ball in the game was goalkeeper Sepp Maier when he picked it out of the back of his net! For the next 25 minutes, Holland played quite breathtaking football, their "Total Football" leaving their opponents hopelessly outclassed as they strode imperiously across the pitch, switching positions at will and not letting the Germans near the ball. Significantly, however, they failed to add to their lead, seemingly concerned more with humiliating their bitter rivals through outplaying them rather than outscoring them. Indeed, midfielder Wim Van Hanegem seemed to confirm this after the match, saying: "I didn't give a damn about the score, 1-0 was enough as long as we could humiliate them." However, on 25 minutes and utterly against the run of play, the Germans finally managed to get hold of the ball and winger Bernd Holzenbein ran into the box before collapsing under Wim Jansen's challenge. Holzenbein had a reputation for diving and whether contact had taken place was dubious at best but Taylor awarded the penalty to the fury of the Dutch. Paul Breitner stepped up and sent Jan Jongbloed the wrong way for 1-1. Holland sought to hit back quickly but Cruyff was not his usual self. Right-back Vogts was man-marking him brilliantly, shackling him so effectively that he could barely get a kick. On the stroke of half-time, holding midfielder Rainer Bonhof crossed from the right for Gerd Muller. The little striker's first touch was not great, knocking the ball away from goal, but in a flash he turned and shot past a shocked Jongbloed. Germany had a 2-1 half-time lead, much to the dismay of the Dutch and the fury of Cruyff, who was so angry he was booked by Taylor for remonstrating with him at length as the players headed for the dressing room.

Holland had to respond in the second period and a return to the dazzling football of earlier in the game would likely have been enough to manage it. However, the players seemed to be following more of a personal vendetta against the Germans than any strict game plan. The legacy of the Second World War had left a deep-rooted hatred of the Germans amongst many of the

> ## Stat Attack
>
> Johan Neesken's penalty was the first spot-kick awarded in a World Cup final. It was scored so early on and after a period of Dutch possession that with the score at 1-0, no German player had touched the ball!

> ## Stat Attack
>
> Gerd Muller's goal in the final was his fourth of the tournament and 14th career World Cup goal, enough to put him clear as the top scorer in the tournament's history, a record he held until Ronaldo scored his 15th World Cup goal against Ghana in 2006.

population of Holland, leaving matches between the two as one of the most fiercely contested rivalries in all of football. Here, the Dutch were far the more talented team but were putting far too much emphasis on their individual skill, seemingly trying to beat the Germans on their own. This was absolutely the opposite of the aim of "Total Football" but falling behind to the team they were most desperate to beat seemed to have rattled them. They had plenty of opportunities to equalise and take the game into extra time but were unable to make use of them, Johnny Rep just failing to reach a cross at the far post with the goal gaping, Maier saving brilliantly from Neeskens' stinging drive and Breitner in the right place to clear one effort off the line. At the death, little Muller again controlled in the area and fired home but the goal was harshly disallowed for offside. Still, it wasn't to matter and Holland were unable to find late salvation. Incredibly, the hugely fancied Dutch had lost in the final and the hosts Germany could celebrate an unexpected triumph on home soil, their second World Cup victory.

World Cup Final result

Holland 1-2 West Germany
07/07/74 – Munich (Olympiastadion)
Holland: Jongbloed, Suurbier, Rijsbergen (De Jong), Haan, Krol, Jansen, Neeskens, Van Hanegem, Rep, Cruyff (c), Rensenbrink (R Van de Kerkhof)
Goals: Neeskens pen 2
West Germany: Maier, Vogts, Schwarzenbeck, Beckenbauer (c), Breitner, Hoeness, Bonhof, Overath, Grabowski, Muller, Holzenbein
Goals: Breitner pen 25, Muller 43
Referee: Taylor (England)

West Germany won the 1974 World Cup.

Tournament awards

Golden Boot: Grzegorz Lato (Poland) – 7 goals
(Runners-up: Andrzej Szarmach (Poland)/Johan Neeskens (Holland) – 5)

Best Player: Johan Cruyff (Holland)

Best Goal: Paul Breitner (West Germany) – Holland scored some staggering team goals in the tournament but it was the hammer-footed German left-back Breitner who scored probably the best goal of the competition against Chile. After some nice build-up play and one-touch football, the ball was worked to Breitner more than 35 yards out from goal on the right but his thunderous drive flew into the top corner.

Star XI:
Goalkeeper – Jan Tomaszewski (Poland)
Defenders – Berti Vogts (West Germany), Franz Beckenbauer (West Germany), Ruud Krol (Holland), Paul Breitner (West Germany)
Midfielders – Johan Neeskens (Holland), Kazimierz Deyna (Poland), Wolfgang Overath (West Germany)
Forwards – Grzegorz Lato (Poland), Johan Cruyff (Holland), Rob Rensenbrink (Holland)

World Cup Great – Franz Beckenbauer (West Germany)

German football has always placed a focus on keeping things tight at the back but at the same time building their attacks through the team and instilling a fierce drive and winning mentality throughout their side. It is perhaps fitting, then, that their greatest ever player, Franz Beckenbauer, was the embodiment of all these characteristics.

The young Beckenbauer grew up in Munich as a fan of 1860 Munich. However, it was the other major side from the city, Bayern, who snapped up a teenage Beckenbauer as he began to make his mark in a local youth side as a composed all-round midfielder. Primarily a holding player, Beckenbauer was physically and aerially dominant and strong in the tackle but it was his reading of the game and footballing brain that really set him apart as something special. He was able to spot danger well ahead of others and this caused him almost always to be in the right place at the right time. Allied to this, he was imperious going forward, a supreme passer and dribbler and possessed of a ferocious shot. Even from a young age, Beckenbauer looked the complete player.

By 1965, the youngster had already established himself as a fixture in the Bayern Munich side and his first international cap would come later the same year, just weeks after his 20th birthday. Beckenbauer's incredible ability and maturity well beyond his tender years saw him become a key part of the side which reached the World Cup final in 1966. Despite being only 20, Beckenbauer turned in a string of eye-catching performances from midfield, bursting onto the international scene in sensational fashion. He scored four goals in the tournament despite having a largely defensive role, most of them after majestic runs forward where he seemed to just glide past players. In the final itself he was assigned to mark Bobby Charlton and he kept England's key player relatively quiet. However, Germany missed his inspiration up the field and went down 4-2 in extra time.

After leading his club to the Bundesliga title in 1969, the "Kaiser" was back as a key part of the West Germany team who finished third in the 1970 World Cup. Adopting a somewhat more defensive role in midfield, Beckenbauer was again at his imperious best. In the quarter-final against England it was his unshakable determination and will to win that lifted his team to unlikely victory, scoring the first goal himself. In the semi-final defeat to Italy, Beckenbauer's incredible fighting spirit was again in evidence; he dislocated his shoulder in the game but played on with his arm in a sling because the Germans had already used both permitted substitutions!

1972 was to prove a golden year for Beckenbauer. By this time he was in his prime and had dropped back into defence, practically inventing the modern sweeper position in the process. By dropping deep, Beckenbauer could use his defensive abilities and reading of the game to snuff out danger and then burst forward or feed accurate passes to his team mates. He was effectively his side's general in the rear. Playing from this position, Beckenbauer captained Bayern to the Bundesliga title and then led his country to triumph in the European Championships in the side still commonly thought of as Germany's best ever. His superb performances for club and country saw him pip Johan Cruyff to the European Footballer of the Year award that season.

The sweeper Beckenbauer was to win two more Bundesliga titles with Bayern in the following seasons and in the latter, 1974, he also led his club to European Cup glory. Weeks later, he was leading his country on home soil at the World Cup. Beckenbauer was one of the two best players of the tournament, conducting play from deep and sweeping up behind his fellow defenders. He effortlessly led the Germans to the final, where they improbably beat Holland. Again, Beckenbauer played a key part, not just for his exceptional performance but again his determination to win was to the fore. He simply would not accept defeat to Germany's great rivals and consequently he became the first captain to hold aloft the new World Cup Trophy.

Beckenbauer led Bayern to three successive European Cups, following victory in 1974 by retaining the trophy the two following years. 1976 would also see him again captain Germany to the final of a major international tournament, the European Championships. Again they were the best team but this time lost on penalties to Czechoslovakia in the final. Still Beckenbauer was named European Footballer of the Year that season but it was the beginning of the end for the great man. He played his last game for both club and country the following year, leaving the international scene with 103 caps. He moved to play in the North American Soccer League, leading New York Cosmos to unprecedented success. After a brief spell back at Hamburg, Beckenbauer retired in 1983.

There was still more to come from Beckenbauer, however. He took his intense will to win into a coaching career, leading a relatively weak West Germany side to the 1986 World Cup final before taking a better side to glory four years later, becoming the only man to win the World Cup both as captain and coach. Later he would be the key figure in the organisation of the 2006 World Cup on home soil. In everything he did, the "Kaiser" always gave 100%. The ultimate winner, Beckenbauer is unquestionably the greatest ever defender and vies with Johan Cruyff for the title of Europe's best ever player.

World Cup Great – Johan Cruyff (Holland)

During the early 1970s, Ajax and Holland perfected a style of play known as "Total Football", which relied upon all-round footballing skills from all the players, superb movement, vision and passing and, above all, a supreme understanding of each player's team mates. Coach Rinus Michels was the inventor but there is no doubt that the key factor behind the system's success for both club and country was the player who coordinated it all: the great Johan Cruyff.

Cruyff came up through the youth ranks at Ajax and made his first appearance for the senior side in 1964, aged 17. The arrival of Michels as coach was to turn the Amsterdam club into Europe's most dominant team and Cruyff quickly developed into the team's natural leader. Cruyff played nominally as the team's centre forward but he more than any of his team mates was the ultimate incarnation of total football, utterly unrestricted by position. He would frequently drift out to the wings to provide crosses, drop back deep to put his foot in in midfield or find himself space to dictate proceedings. His almost telepathic understanding of his team mates' movement allowed him to feed them with pinpoint passes and effortlessly control the game, at the same time carrying a potent all-round goal threat himself. With a young Cruyff in top form, Ajax reached the European Cup Final in 1969 but were beaten by AC Milan.

Defeat was not to matter for Cruyff and Ajax, however, as they would have several more appearances in European club football's biggest match. Cruyff and his team utterly dominated the competition in the early 1970s, winning the trophy three times in a row between 1971 and 1973. In the 1972 tournament, their opponents were Inter Milan, boasting their famed "Catenaccio" defensive system. However, Cruyff and his team mates put in perhaps the defining performance of "Total Football", exposing the Italian system as far too rigid as they swept them aside. Cruyff, wearing his famed number 14 shirt, was the inspiration and key player in all three victories and his brilliance saw him crowned European Footballer of the Year in 1971 and 1973.

In the same year as Cruyff led Ajax to their third successive European Cup, he decided to link up with his former coach Michels, who was now at Barcelona. Cruyff's performances for his new club were no less spectacular than for Ajax. In his first season, 1973-74, he helped them win the league title, again being the creative hub of another club following the "Total Football" model.

1974 would also see Cruyff's only chance to shine with his national side at a World Cup. Captain and leader just as he was for his club, Cruyff was unquestionably the player of the tournament as Holland's "Total Football" proved altogether too much for their opponents. Cruyff controlled the carnage effortlessly and scored three goals himself as well as unveiling his trademark "Cruyff turn" to gasps of amazement. Holland effortlessly strode into the final where hosts and archenemies Germany were waiting. On the day, Holland sensationally took the lead in the opening seconds but thereafter seemed too set on humiliating their opponents rather than simply beating them. It proved a mistake as Germany incredibly recovered to win 2-1. Cruyff and his side are regarded by many as the greatest team never to have won the World Cup. Hungary's 1954 unit are probably the only others who come close.

Despite defeat in the final, Cruyff retained the European Footballer of the Year that season and is one of only three players to win the prestigious award on three occasions. He continued to star with Barcelona and should have had another chance at World Cup glory in 1978 but he opted out of travelling to the tournament. It was generally considered at the time that he did so to protest against the fascist government of Argentina, where the tournament was held, but various theories have been put forward, including that he was banned by his wife after a team party got out of hand in the 1974 tournament.

The same year as his former team mates were competing in the tournament, Cruyff decided to play out the twilight of his career in the North American Soccer League. However, Ajax's favourite son would return to his original club in 1981 before finishing his career at their rivals Feyenoord in 1984. Cruyff continued his maverick free-thinking into management, with a highly successful spell at Ajax before an even better one as coach of the "Dream Team" of the early 90s at Barcelona, becoming their most successful ever coach with a string of trophies, including winning the European Cup in 1992, ensuring he had won the trophy both as a player and as a manager.

Few players throughout history have been as naturally gifted at football as Cruyff. A complete footballer with great pace, outstanding technical ability and fabulously accurate passing, it was nevertheless his understanding of his team mates that made him the world's best player in the early 1970s. Sometimes aloof off the field, Cruyff's unique ability stemmed from him combining his natural talent with his visionary thinking on and off the field. As he himself described it: "Football is a game you play with your head." With his combination of incredible skill and freethinking genius, Cruyff is widely considered the best ever footballer born in Europe.

World Cup Great – Gerd Muller (West Germany)

There can have been few football players who looked quite so ungainly as Germany's striker Gerd Muller. Short and stocky, he seemed to lumber around the pitch, utterly devoid of the grace normally associated with great players. However, even among some of the world's greatest ever strikers, almost no-one can match Muller's incredible goalscoring record for every side he ever played for. He was the ultimate proof that appearances can be deceptive.

Muller started his career at his local club 1861 Nordlingen in Bavaria. However, after just one season there at senior level, he left for another Bavarian side, Bayern Munich, as an 18-year-old in 1964. Initially, Muller was left on the fringes of the first team, as the coaching staff, deceived by his short stature and clumsy-looking movement, didn't see him as much of a player, despite the number of goals he had scored at Nordlingen. However, soon Muller's sheer weight of goals forced them to change their minds and see Muller rightfully as the team's key striker. The ultimate penalty-box predator, Muller was a prolific goal scorer who in a split-second could turn a half chance into a goal. His incredible scoring feats would see him finish as the Bundesliga's top scorer on seven occasions, including on all four occasions the club won the title during Muller's stay.

International recognition for Muller first came in 1966, when he made his debut for West Germany in the aftermath of his country's loss to England in the World Cup final. By the time of the 1970 tournament in Mexico, Muller was firmly established as the nation's number one striker and he showed exactly why. Notching hat-tricks in successive games in the group phase, Muller achieved a remarkable ten goals in the tournament, the third highest tally ever for a single tournament and the only time so many goals have been scored in a single World Cup in the modern era. The manner of Muller's goals may not have been spectacular, all coming from inside the box, but the sheer number certainly was. Muller's performances saw him named European Footballer of the Year that season.

Muller boasts an incredible record of scoring in major finals. Bayern Munich won the European Cup in three successive seasons between 1974 and 1976 and Muller scored three times in the finals to help his side to victory. The goal poacher extraordinaire also scored twice in the final to help West Germany win the 1972 European Championships before saving the most important for the 1974 World Cup on home soil. Despite not being at his best at the tournament, Muller had already scored three times to help West Germany to the final against Holland. There, with the score poised at 1-1, he scored the winner, his 14th career World Cup goal, a record he held until Brazilian star Ronaldo broke it in 2006.

The winner in the World Cup final would prove to be Muller's last ever international goal as he never played for his country again. However, he left international football with a remarkable record of 68 goals in just 62 games, a strike rate that is all but unmatched by footballers who have earned more than 50 caps. Indeed, no player since the late 50s has come close to Muller's incredible scoring records. In the early days, with fewer defenders and less emphasis on tactics, goals were much easier to come by. Muller's outstanding feats in the modern era are unique.

Muller left Bayern in 1979 to play out his final two seasons in the North American Soccer League, again notching plenty of goals. Not the prettiest player to watch by any means, there is no doubt that in many ways Muller was a very limited footballer: not particularly quick and with very little ability outside the box, he carried precious little threat in two thirds of the pitch. However, arguably no other footballer was as deadly with the ball at his feet in the area as little Muller. With incredibly composed and accurate finishing with either foot and remarkable ability in the air for a man of such short stature, Muller was an unrivalled goal poacher. His low centre of gravity also allowed him to turn in an instant, making him at his most dangerous when the defenders thought they had him under wraps. Muller may have never scored a truly spectacular goal in his entire career but almost no other player in the last 40 years has scored as many goals as "The Bomber." They all count the same anyway!

Few expected it beforehand but Holland, by far the best team in the tournament, had fallen at the last hurdle to the hosts West Germany. Undoubtedly the best team in the tournament, the Dutch were desperately unlucky not to carry off the trophy they so richly deserved. However, they were victims of their own passion in the final, allowing the feelings of hatred and superiority towards the Germans felt by many of the squad to cloud their play and let the Germans back into their game. There is no doubt, however, that over their seven matches they were the best team in the tournament – some would say the best in any tournament – and for them not to carry off the trophy at the end of it was a huge shock.

Nevertheless, those who claim the West Germans were unworthy winners do no justice at all to an exceptional team. Of course, the fact it was again the Germans who beat the tournament's star team, as they had done to Hungary in 1954, meant parallels were inevitably drawn but really the only justified one here would be that both Hungary and Holland were exceptional sides. Whereas the Germans' 1954 team were for the most part unexceptional and desperately lucky to finish the tournament as champions, their 1974 vintage was packed with world-class players and were certainly one of the two best teams in the competition. Cruyff and Neeskens had lit up the tournament for Holland but so had the likes of Beckenbauer, Overath, Maier and Muller amongst others for the Germans. Certainly home advantage and a kind second-round draw helped but there could be no argument that West Germany 1974 were anything but worthy winners of the tournament.

The only other team who could be truly proud of their achievements in the competition were Poland. Finishing third having participated in just one World Cup match prior to the tournament, they came with absolutely no experience but proved themselves a quality side. Winning all five of their first games, they were also, like the Dutch, one of the few teams committed to attacking football. That they had provided several of the tournament's stars only increased the feeling that they were more than worthy winners of the bronze medal and indeed were somewhat unfortunate not to make it to the final itself.

Elsewhere, however, 1974 was not a vintage year for the World Cup. There was no doubt the bad luck of the competition being played almost exclusively in terrible weather contributed at times to the poor spectacle but the major problem was that, after the thrills of 1970, most of the teams returned to a defensive game revolving around stopping the opposition rather than making play themselves. Saddest of all was that holders Brazil, who had played such glorious football to win in 1970, were themselves drawn into this tactic and were a shadow of the glorious side the world had fallen in love with just four years earlier. For some there had been bad luck, most notably for Scotland, who left the tournament the only team undefeated. For most, however, including the neutrals watching on, the World Cup of 1974 was largely a disappointment. The glorious play of the Dutch and the cavalier attitude of the Poles certainly caught the eye but elsewhere there was precious little to get the blood pumping. It was hoped that the tournament's return to South America in four years time would also see a return to the attacking ways of 1970.

1978: Argentina

Qualification

107 Entrants.
West Germany qualified as holders.
Argentina qualified as hosts.

Europe

Group 1

Cyprus 1-5 Denmark, Portugal 0-2 Poland, Denmark 5-0 Cyprus, Poland 5-0 Cyprus, Portugal 1-0 Denmark, Cyprus 1-2 Portugal, Denmark 1-2 Poland, Cyprus 1-3 Poland, Poland 4-1 Denmark, Denmark 2-4 Portugal, Poland 1-1 Portugal, Portugal 4-0 Cyprus

	Pld	W	D	L	GF	GA	Pts
Poland	6	5	1	0	17	4	11
Portugal	6	4	1	1	12	6	9
Denmark	6	2	0	4	14	12	4
Cyprus	6	0	0	6	3	24	0

Poland qualified.

Group 2

Finland 1-4 England, Finland 7-1 Luxembourg, England 2-1 Finland, Luxembourg 1-4 Italy, Italy 2-0 England, England 5-0 Luxembourg, Luxembourg 0-1 Finland, Finland 0-3 Italy, Luxembourg 0-2 England, Italy 6-1 Finland, England 2-0 Italy, Italy 3-0 Luxembourg

	Pld	W	D	L	GF	GA	Pts
Italy	6	5	0	1	18	4	10
England	6	5	0	1	15	4	10
Finland	6	2	0	4	11	16	4
Luxembourg	6	0	0	6	2	22	0

Italy qualified.

Group 3

Turkey 4-0 Malta, East Germany 1-1 Turkey, Malta 0-1 Austria, Malta 0-1 East Germany, Austria 1-0 Turkey, Austria 9-0 Malta, Austria 1-1 East Germany, East Germany 1-1 Austria, East Germany 9-0 Malta, Turkey 0-1 Austria, Turkey 1-2 East Germany, Malta 0-3 Turkey

	Pld	W	D	L	GF	GA	Pts
Austria	6	4	2	0	14	2	10
East Germany	6	3	3	0	15	4	9
Turkey	6	2	1	3	9	5	5
Malta	6	0	0	6	0	27	0

Austria qualified.

Group 4

Iceland 0-1 Belgium, Iceland 0-1 Holland, Holland 2-2 Northern Ireland, Belgium 2-0 Northern Ireland, Belgium 0-2 Holland, Iceland 1-0 Northern Ireland, Holland 4-1 Iceland, Belgium 4-0 Iceland, Northern Ireland 2-0 Iceland, Northern Ireland 0-1 Holland, Holland 1-0 Belgium, Northern Ireland 3-0 Belgium

	Pld	W	D	L	GF	GA	Pts
Holland	6	5	1	0	11	3	11
Belgium	6	3	0	3	7	6	6
Northern Ireland	6	2	1	3	7	6	5
Iceland	6	1	0	5	2	12	2

Holland qualified.

Group 5

Bulgaria 2-2 France, France 2-0 Republic of Ireland, Republic of Ireland 1-0 France, Bulgaria 2-1 Republic of Ireland, Republic of Ireland 0-0 Bulgaria, France 3-1 Bulgaria

	Pld	W	D	L	GF	GA	Pts
France	4	2	1	1	7	4	5
Bulgaria	4	1	2	1	5	6	4
Republic of Ireland	4	1	1	2	2	4	3

France qualified.

Group 6

Sweden 2-0 Norway, Norway 1-0 Switzerland, Switzerland 1-2 Sweden, Sweden 2-1 Switzerland, Norway 2-1 Sweden, Switzerland 1-0 Norway

	Pld	W	D	L	GF	GA	Pts
Sweden	4	3	0	1	7	4	6
Norway	4	2	0	2	3	4	4
Switzerland	4	1	0	3	3	5	2

Sweden qualified.

Group 7

Czechoslovakia 2-0 Scotland, Scotland 1-0 Wales, Wales 3-0 Czechoslovakia, Scotland 3-1 Czechoslovakia, Wales 0-2 Scotland (in England), Czechoslovakia 1-0 Wales

	Pld	W	D	L	GF	GA	Pts
Scotland	4	3	0	1	6	3	6
Czechoslovakia	4	2	0	2	4	6	4
Wales	4	1	0	3	3	4	2

Scotland qualified.

Group 8

Spain 1-0 Yugoslavia, Romania 1-0 Spain, Yugoslavia 0-2 Romania, Spain 2-0 Romania, Romania 4-6 Yugoslavia, Yugoslavia 0-1 Spain

	Pld	W	D	L	GF	GA	Pts
Spain	4	3	0	1	4	1	6
Romania	4	2	0	2	7	8	4
Yugoslavia	4	1	0	3	6	8	2

Spain qualified.

Group 9

Greece 1-1 Hungary, USSR 2-0 Greece, Hungary 2-1 USSR, Greece 1-0 USSR, USSR 2-0 Hungary, Hungary 3-0 Greece

	Pld	W	D	L	GF	GA	Pts
Hungary	4	2	1	1	6	4	5
USSR	4	2	0	2	5	3	4
Greece	4	1	1	2	2	6	3

Hungary qualified for UEFA/CONMEBOL play-off.

South America

First Round

Group 1

Colombia 0-0 Brazil, Colombia 0-1 Paraguay, Paraguay 1-1 Colombia, Brazil 6-0 Colombia, Paraguay 0-1 Brazil, Brazil 1-1 Paraguay

	Pld	W	D	L	GF	GA	Pts
Brazil	4	2	2	0	8	1	6
Paraguay	4	1	2	1	3	3	4
Colombia	4	0	2	2	1	8	2

Brazil qualified for final round.

Group 2

Venezuela 1-1 Uruguay, Bolivia 1-0 Uruguay, Venezuela 1-3 Bolivia, Bolivia 2-0 Venezuela, Uruguay 2-0 Venezuela, Uruguay 2-2 Bolivia

	Pld	W	D	L	GF	GA	Pts
Bolivia	4	3	1	0	8	3	7
Uruguay	4	1	2	1	5	4	4
Venezuela	4	0	1	3	2	8	1

Bolivia qualified for final round.

Group 3

Ecuador 1-1 Peru, Ecuador 0-1 Chile, Chile 1-1 Peru, Peru 4-0 Ecuador, Chile 3-0 Ecuador, Peru 2-0 Chile

	Pld	W	D	L	GF	GA	Pts
Peru	4	2	2	0	8	2	6
Chile	4	2	1	1	5	3	5
Ecuador	4	0	1	3	1	9	1

Peru qualified for final round.

Final Round (in Colombia)

Brazil 1-0 Peru, Brazil 8-0 Bolivia, Peru 5-0 Bolivia

	Pld	W	D	L	GF	GA	Pts
Brazil	2	2	0	0	9	0	4
Peru	2	1	0	1	5	1	2
Bolivia	2	0	0	2	0	13	0

Brazil and **Peru** qualified, Bolivia to UEFA/CONMEBOL play-off.

UEFA/CONMEBOL Play-off

Hungary v Bolivia: 6-0, 3-2 (agg. 9-2)

Hungary qualified.

North and Central America

North American Zone

Canada 1-1 USA, USA 0-0 Mexico, Canada 1-0 Mexico, Mexico 3-0 USA, USA 2-0 Canada, Mexico 0-0 Canada

	Pld	W	D	L	GF	GA	Pts
Mexico	4	1	2	1	3	1	4
USA	4	1	2	1	3	4	4
Canada	4	1	2	1	2	3	4

Play-off (in Haiti): Canada 3-0 USA

Mexico and Canada qualified for final round.

Central American Zone

Honduras withdrew.
Panama 3-2 Costa Rica, Panama 1-1 El Salvador, Costa Rica 3-0 Panama, El Salvador 4-1 Panama, Panama 2-4 Guatemala, Guatemala 7-0 Panama, El Salvador 1-1 Costa Rica, Costa Rica 0-0 Guatemala, Guatemala 3-1 El Salvador, Guatemala 1-1 Costa Rica, Costa Rica 1-1 El Salvador, El Salvador 2-0 Guatemala

	Pld	W	D	L	GF	GA	Pts
Guatemala	6	3	2	1	15	6	8
El Salvador	6	2	3	1	10	7	7
Costa Rica	6	1	4	1	8	6	6
Panama	6	1	1	4	7	21	3

Guatemala and El Salvador qualified for final round.

Caribbean Zone

Preliminary Round

Dominican Republic v Haiti: 0-3, 0-3 (agg. 0-6)

Haiti qualified for first round.

First Round

Guyana v Suriname: 2-0, 0-3 (agg. 2-3)
Barbados v Trinidad and Tobago: 2-1, 0-1 (agg. 2-2), Play-off (in Barbados): Barbados 1-3 Trinidad and Tobago
Dutch Antilles v Haiti: 1-2, 0-7 (agg. 1-9)
Jamaica v Cuba: 1-3, 0-2 (agg. 1-5)

Suriname, Trinidad and Tobago, Haiti and Cuba qualified for second round.

Second Round

Suriname v Trinidad and Tobago: 1-1, 2-2 (agg. 3-3), Play-off (in French Guiana): Suriname 3-2 Trinidad and Tobago (aet)
Cuba v Haiti: 1-1, 1-1 (agg. 2-2), Play-off (in Panama): Haiti 2-0 Cuba

Suriname and Haiti qualified for final round.

Final Round (in Mexico)

Guatemala 3-2 Suriname, El Salvador 2-1 Canada, Mexico 4-1 Haiti, Mexico 3-1 El Salvador, Canada 2-1 Suriname, Haiti 2-1 Guatemala, Mexico 8-1 Suriname, Canada 2-1 Guatemala, Haiti 1-0 El Salvador, Mexico 2-1 Guatemala, El Salvador 3-2 Suriname, Canada 1-1 Haiti, Mexico 3-1 Canada, Haiti 1-0 Suriname, Guatemala 2-2 El Salvador

	Pld	W	D	L	GF	GA	Pts
Mexico	5	5	0	0	20	5	10
Haiti	5	3	1	1	6	6	7
El Salvador	5	2	1	2	8	9	5
Canada	5	2	1	2	7	8	5
Guatemala	5	1	1	3	8	10	3
Suriname	5	0	0	5	6	17	0

Mexico qualified.

96

Africa

Preliminary Round

Sierra Leone v Niger: 5-1, 1-2 (agg. 6-3)
Upper Volta v Mauritania: 1-1, 2-0 (agg. 3-1)

Sierra Leone and Upper Volta qualified for first round.

First Round

Algeria v Libya: 1-0, 0-0 (agg. 1-0)
Zambia v Malawi: 4-0, 1-0 (agg. 5-0)
Upper Volta v Ivory Coast: 1-1, 0-2 (agg. 1-3)
Ghana v Guinea: 2-1, 1-2 (agg. 3-3), Play-off (in Togo): Guinea 2-0 Ghana
Sierra Leone v Nigeria: 0-0, 2-6 (agg. 2-6)
Togo v Senegal: 1-0, 1-1 (agg. 2-1)
Congo v Cameroon: 2-2, 2-1 (match abandoned after rioting) (agg. 4-3)
Egypt v Ethiopia: 3-0, 2-1 (agg. 5-1)
Morocco v Tunisia: 1-1, 1-1 (aet) (agg. 2-2, Tunisia won 4-2 on penalties)
Sudan v Kenya: Sudan withdrew, Kenya received bye.
Central African Empire v Zaire: CAE withdrew, Zaire received bye.
Tanzania v Uganda: Tanzania withdrew, Uganda received bye.

Algeria, Zambia, Ivory Coast, Guinea, Nigeria, Togo, Congo, Egypt, Tunisia, Kenya, Zaire and Uganda qualified for second round.

Second Round

Kenya v Egypt: 0-0, 0-1 (agg. 0-1)
Tunisia v Algeria: 2-0, 1-1 (agg. 3-1)
Ivory Coast v Congo: 3-2, 3-1 (agg. 6-3)
Togo v Guinea: 0-2, 1-2 (agg. 1-4)
Uganda v Zambia: 1-0, 2-4 (aet) (agg. 3-4)
Zaire v Nigeria: Zaire withdrew, Nigeria received bye.

Egypt, Tunisia, Ivory Coast, Guinea, Zambia and Nigeria qualified for third round.

Third Round

Guinea v Tunisia: 1-0, 1-3 (agg. 2-3)
Nigeria v Ivory Coast: 4-0, 2-2 (agg. 6-2)
Egypt v Zambia: 2-0, 0-0 (agg. 2-0)

Tunisia, Nigeria and Egypt qualified for final round.

Final Round

Tunisia 0-0 Nigeria, Nigeria 4-0 Egypt, Egypt 3-1 Nigeria, Nigeria 0-1 Tunisia, Egypt 3-2 Tunisia, Tunisia 4-1 Egypt

	Pld	W	D	L	GF	GA	Pts
Tunisia	4	2	1	1	7	4	5
Egypt	4	2	0	2	7	11	4
Nigeria	4	1	1	2	5	4	3

Tunisia qualified.

Asia and Oceania

First Round

South Vietnam were conquered by North Vietnam and forced to withdraw.

Group 1 (in Singapore)

Sri Lanka withdrew.
Singapore 2-0 Thailand, Hong Kong 4-1 Indonesia, Malaysia 6-4 Thailand, Singapore 2-2 Hong Kong, Indonesia 0-0 Malaysia, Hong Kong 2-1 Thailand, Singapore 1-0 Malaysia, Thailand 3-2 Indonesia, Hong Kong 1-1 Malaysia, Singapore 0-4 Indonesia

	Pld	W	D	L	GF	GA	Pts
Hong Kong	4	2	2	0	9	5	6
Singapore	4	2	1	1	5	6	5
Malaysia	4	1	2	1	7	6	4
Indonesia	4	1	1	2	7	7	3
Thailand	4	1	0	3	8	12	2

Play-off: Singapore 0-1 Hong Kong

Hong Kong qualified for final round.

Group 2

North Korea withdrew.
Israel 0-0 South Korea, Israel 2-0 Japan, Japan 0-2 Israel (in Israel), South Korea 3-1 Israel, Japan 0-0 South Korea, South Korea 1-0 Japan

	Pld	W	D	L	GF	GA	Pts
South Korea	4	2	2	0	4	1	6
Israel	4	2	1	1	5	3	5
Japan	4	0	1	3	0	5	1

South Korea qualified for final round.

Group 3

Iraq withdrew.

Saudi Arabia 2-0 Syria, Syria 2-1 Saudi Arabia, Saudi Arabia 0-3 Iran, Syria 0-1 Iran, Iran 2-0 Syria (Syria forfeited match, Iran awarded 2-0 win), Iran 2-0 Saudi Arabia

	Pld	W	D	L	GF	GA	Pts
Iran	4	4	0	0	8	0	8
Saudi Arabia	4	1	0	3	3	7	2
Syria	4	1	0	3	2	6	2

Iran qualified for final round.

Group 4 (in Qatar)

United Arab Emirates withdrew.

Kuwait 2-0 Bahrain, Qatar 2-0 Bahrain, Qatar 0-2 Kuwait, Kuwait 2-1 Bahrain, Qatar 0-3 Bahrain, Qatar 1-4 Kuwait

	Pld	W	D	L	GF	GA	Pts
Kuwait	4	4	0	0	10	2	8
Bahrain	4	1	0	3	4	6	2
Qatar	4	1	0	3	3	9	2

Kuwait qualified for final round.

Group 5

Australia 3-0 Taiwan (in Fiji), Taiwan 1-2 Australia (in Fiji), New Zealand 6-0 Taiwan, Taiwan 0-6 New Zealand (in New Zealand), Australia 3-1 New Zealand, New Zealand 1-1 Australia

	Pld	W	D	L	GF	GA	Pts
Australia	4	3	1	0	9	3	7
New Zealand	4	2	1	1	14	4	5
Taiwan	4	0	0	4	1	17	0

Australia qualified for final round.

Final Round

Hong Kong 0-2 Iran, Hong Kong 0-1 South Korea, South Korea 0-0 Iran, Australia 3-0 Hong Kong, Australia 0-1 Iran, Australia 2-1 South Korea, Hong Kong 1-3 Kuwait, South Korea 1-0 Kuwait, Australia 1-2 Kuwait, South Korea 0-0 Australia, Iran 1-0 Kuwait, Hong Kong 2-5 Australia, Kuwait 2-2 South Korea, Iran 2-2 South Korea, Kuwait 4-0 Hong Kong, Iran 3-0 Hong Kong, Kuwait 1-0 Australia, Iran 1-0 Australia, Kuwait 1-2 Iran, South Korea 5-2 Hong Kong

	Pld	W	D	L	GF	GA	Pts
Iran	8	6	2	0	12	3	14
South Korea	8	3	4	1	12	8	10
Kuwait	8	4	1	3	13	8	9
Australia	8	3	1	4	11	8	7
Hong Kong	8	0	0	8	5	26	0

Iran qualified.

The Contenders

Argentina	Mexico
Austria	Peru
Brazil	Poland
France	Scotland
Holland	Spain
Hungary	Sweden
Iran	Tunisia
Italy	West Germany

Argentina, a country which had failed several times previously in its bid to host the tournament, finally won the right to host the World Cup in 1978. However, it had sadly coincided with the rise to power of a brutal military Junta dictatorship which murdered its opponents and was widely condemned for human rights abuses. Unsurprisingly given this atmosphere, there was somewhat of a sombre air going into the tournament. This was not helped by the fact that there looked to be no real standout teams in the competition. Even those who had impressed in 1974 appeared to be coming with considerably weaker teams and most of the top nations were in the process of rebuilding their sides, boasting a mix of ageing veterans and untested youngsters. It didn't bode well for a tournament of high quality football.

The experiment with a second group phase, which had garnered a mixed reception in Germany four years earlier, was retained, meaning again that a knockout system would only exist for the final itself and the third-place play-off. However, a new innovation had been brought in in the form of the penalty shootout, a hugely controversial means to decide games when two teams remained level after extra time. Two years earlier it had seen Czechoslovakia crowned European Champions ahead of West Germany and it had already been used in qualifying to see eventual qualifiers Tunisia edge past Morocco.

By far the toughest looking group seemed to be Group One, where hosts **Argentina** would play in River Plate's Monumental stadium in the capital Buenos Aires. Chainsmoking coach Cesar Luis Menotti had been tasked with leading the hosts to glory and at least he could count on some talented players, many of whom had been blooded successfully in Germany 1974. Valencia star Mario Kempes looked to be the key player, able to play either as a conventional centre forward or in a more withdrawn role where he could cause havoc running from deep. Assisting him would be several talented players, including winger Rene Houseman, versatile midfielder Osvaldo Ardiles, composed sweeper and captain Daniel Passarella and solid goalkeeper Ubaldo Fillol. With the added benefit of their passionate home support, they would undoubtedly mount a strong challenge.

Keeping them company were a fine **Italy** side, who looked to have rebuilt well following the disappointment of 1974. They had just managed to edge out England by the skin of their teeth to qualify and now Enzo Bearzot's team would be eager to make their presence felt. Boasting an uncompromising defence controlled by impenetrable keeper Dino Zoff and featuring the likes of his Juventus team mates Claudio Gentile, Gaetano Scirea and Antonio Cabrini as well as the tough Mauro Bellugi, they would be next to impossible to score against, especially considering the screening presence of Marco Tardelli and Romeo Benetti in midfield. The Azzurri boasted impressive creative options too, with playmakers Franco Causio and Giancarlo Antognoni looking to feed sharp strikers Paolo Rossi and Roberto Bettega. They seemed to have quality running throughout their squad and were one of the favourites for the title.

France, meanwhile, had returned from their lengthy spell in the footballing doldrums since their class of 1958 and this time, unlike the poor crop of 1966, this generation of youngsters promised much. Their youth and inexperience would no doubt handicap them in a tough group but several of the players were more than capable of stepping up to the challenge. Foremost amongst them was brilliant playmaker Michel Platini, only 23 but seemingly with the world at his feet. Other promising youngsters around him included forwards Dominique Rocheteau, Didier Six and Bernard Lacombe, while the likes of Marius Tresor and Maxime Bossis would keep things tight at the back. Though the young squad were unlikely to win the tournament and were there primarily to learn, their level of natural talent was still such that they would likely have a big say on proceedings.

The fourth member of a formidable quartet were **Hungary**, who like France were playing in their first World Cup since 1966. They too would be no pushovers, though their squad looked solid rather than exceptional and they would likely struggle against three tough opponents. Their key man would likely be star midfielder Tibor Nyilasi, a fine playmaker, while Sandor Gujdar in goal and Andras Torocsik up front would serve as useful book-ends.

Holders **West Germany** had been drawn in Group Two, which would take place primarily in the cities of Rosario and Cordoba. Helmut Schon, going into his fourth World Cup as coach, would have to do without many of his key players from the triumphant 1974 team but still, even though they were in the process of rebuilding, the Germans as always came with a chance. The tigerish Berti Vogts was still there at the heart of the defence, as was keeper Sepp Maier behind him, while young Karl-Heinz Rummenigge was making a name for himself at Bayern Munich as an outstanding striker or right winger. As always, they would fight with characteristic German grit and determination and they certainly couldn't be ruled out.

Poland joined them and would hope to build on their fabulous third place last time around. They came boasting the core of the side who had done so brilliantly in Germany, including midfielder Kazimierz Deyna, winger Grzegorz Lato and striker Andrzej Szarmach, while star forward Wlodzimierz Lubanski, who had missed the 1974 tournament through injury, would finally get the opportunity to show why many considered him the best player in the side. Poland could also boast an outrageously talented young midfielder in Zbigniew Boniek, who came with bags of potential and only strengthened the Poles' already formidable line-up. Matching or even bettering their achievements in 1974 looked a real possibility.

Mexico also returned to the competition, having missed out on the 1974 tournament, though they, like Haiti before them, had been significantly helped by the CONCACAF championship, which doubled as the region's World Cup qualifying tournament, being hosted in their own country.

Still, striker Victor Rangel had been prolific in that tournament and in the teenage Hugo Sanchez he had an outrageously gifted young strike partner. All the same, Mexico's largely young and inexperienced squad would find the going tough against such European heavyweights as West Germany and Poland.

Completing the group were Africa's representatives **Tunisia**, who had qualified after beating Morocco on a penalty shootout. Their squad came with almost no experience of playing football at the top level and unsurprisingly were expected to struggle. They hoped, however, to at least do better in this their debut tournament than fellow Africans Zaire had in their horror show four years earlier.

Generally regarded as favourites, **Brazil** were the most fancied side in Group Three, though their first act in the tournament was to complain that their rivals Argentina had deliberately ensured they played their games at chilly Mar del Plata rather than one of the warmer venues (as the tournament was held in the Southern Hemisphere, it took place during the Argentinean winter). They still were focused sadly on the defensive football they exhibited in Germany in 1974 but at least they were starting to get some attacking swagger back and would certainly be among the strongest of opponents. Veteran playmaker Rivelino remained and he was joined in the creative department by a young and extravagantly gifted attacking midfielder named Zico. With the dangerous Dirceu completing a formidable creative trio, Brazil looked highly capable going forward, although they seemed to be lacking a top-class striker. Further back, Emerson Leao would again keep goal while Edinho would be at the centre of defence, with Toninho Cerezo protecting him from the midfield. They might not have been the most attractive Brazil side ever but they certainly seemed capable of doing the business and would surely be a threat in the competition's latter stages.

Spain were another returning European side who, like France and Hungary, were in their first World Cup since 1966. They had done fantastically to edge out Romania and Yugoslavia in qualifying and now would enjoy being back on the world stage, where they would no doubt receive significant support from the locals. Veteran centre back or midfielder Pirri, the sole survivor from their 1966 team, remained and he would be backed up by the tough Migueli. Further forward, the skills of tricky Real Madrid youngster Juanito would likely be to the fore. Inexperienced, Spain still had the ability to make progress in the tournament.

Also in the group would be **Sweden**, who had impressed in flashes in 1974. This time, however, there was much less cause for Scandinavian optimism. Several of the old heads of that side remained but key striker Ralf Edstrom was not in the best of form while many of the Swedes' other players were at the veteran stage, particularly centre-back Bjorn Nordqvist and midfield warrior Bo Larsson. They were widely expected to struggle.

Rounding out the group were **Austria**, playing in their first World Cup for 20 years after just pipping East Germany in qualifying. They came with genuine hope and seemed to have all the makings of a fine side. The Austrians looked tight at the back, with keeper Friedrich Koncilia controlling a back line which included the various talents of Bruno Pezzey, Robert Sara and Erich Obermayer, with Herbert Prohaska a gifted playmaker in the middle of the park and Hans Krankl, who had smashed six goals past Malta in qualifying, a deadly cutting edge.

Finally, Group Four would be played in the neighbouring western cities of Cordoba and

> ## Only at the World Cup
>
> There have been plenty of theories as to why Johan Cruyff decided not to play in Argentina 1978. At the time many believed he had boycotted it in protest of Argentina's brutal fascist regime but Cruyff himself would later suggest he was rattled following a kidnap attempt on him and his family a year earlier. Others, meanwhile, have suggested that his wife banned him because of his involvement in a party in West Germany 1974 involving players and local women frolicking naked in a swimming pool.

Mendoza and featured **Holland** as its most fancied team. The Dutch were not a side of the calibre of four years earlier. Although several of that glorious team remained, they were past their best and were further hampered by the absence of their star player Johan Cruyff, who declined to travel. Still, with legendary Austrian Ernst Happel at the helm, they still had a side full of world-class players. Johan Neeskens would be exceptional as ever in midfield, Ruud Krol would move from his normal left-back position into the heart of defence as a sweeper while Rob Rensenbrink would, in the absence of Cruyff, who had so often overshadowed him, seek to put himself forward as the team's attacking star. With the talented Van de Kerkhof twins, Rene and Willy, now ready to take on a more full-time role in the team, Holland still came with as good a chance as anyone.

The Dutch were expected to face a stiff challenge in their group from **Scotland**. Keeping the core nucleus of their side from 1974, they boasted quality throughout the team, most notably brilliant Liverpool striker Kenny Dalglish, while his club team mate Graeme Souness was a fantastic all-round midfielder. Manager Ally MacLeod had even gone as far as to state his belief that Scotland were capable of winning the tournament and would return having finished at least in the top three places. Expectation fuelled by his bold comments, the Tartan Army travelled in their thousands and the Scots firmly believed that this would be their year.

Joining these two were **Peru**, who could still boast several of the stars who had caused such a stir in Mexico 1970, even if the majority were now grizzled veterans. Among them was the fantastic midfielder Teofilo Cubillas and the composed defender Hector Chumpitaz, while keeper Ramon Quiroga, famous for spending almost as much time outside his box as in it, certainly lived up to his nickname of "El Loco" (The Crazy One).

Lastly came Asian champions **Iran**, who had qualified impressively ahead of the likes of South Korea and Australia. They would certainly enjoy the adventure but to make further progress would be a huge long shot.

Debutants: Iran, Tunisia

The Draw

Group 1
Argentina
Hungary
France
Italy

Group 2
West Germany
Poland
Mexico
Tunisia

Group 3
Brazil
Sweden
Spain
Austria

Group 4
Holland
Iran
Peru
Scotland

Venues:

Buenos Aires – Monumental, Buenos Aires – Jose Amalfitani, Cordoba, Mar del Plata, Mendoza, Rosario

The Tournament – 1-25 June

Group Stage – First series

The tournament opened at the Estadio Monunmental in Buenos Aires, where the wildly excited Argentinean public crammed in to catch a glimpse of the reigning champions **West Germany** taking on **Poland**. The clash promised much, especially considering both teams had finished in the top three places at the previous tournament, but inevitably the big occasion got to both sides and both seemed paralysed by the terror of defeat. Poland were probably the better side, inspired by the returning Lubanski, and Lato should have scored with a presentable opportunity but it was the Germans who came the closest to breaking the deadlock, Rainer Bonhof firing against the bar. By the end, however, both sides looked uninspired and bereft of ideas. It was a woeful opening to the tournament.

While the opening game had not produced a goal in 90 minutes of sterile football, **Italy**'s grudge match with **France** in Group One produced one after barely 30 seconds. That was all the time it took for Didier Six to burst down the left wing and cross for Bernard Lacombe to head into the corner. The crowd were stunned but the Italians immediately began the search for an equaliser. Striker Paolo Rossi was a constant threat with his silky running and it was he who scored the leveller after a ridiculous goalmouth scramble. A long cross from the right evaded the French defenders and when the ball was pulled back across it was clipped to Franco Causio. His shot came back off a post straight to Rossi but the striker fired his initial effort against Causio's legs before eventually finding the back of the net at the second attempt. The French, however, were undeterred and sought to retake the lead. Twice Michel Platini was somewhat unfortunate to have penalty appeals turned down after he appeared to be brought to ground in the area before the Italians managed to take the lead with ten minutes of the second half gone. Claudio Gentile crossed from the right and substitute Renato Zaccarelli controlled and slotted the ball into the corner on the turn past stunned keeper Jean-Paul Bertrand-Demanes. France had opportunities to equalise late on but couldn't take them. They had slumped to defeat, though they had played well enough to suggest that all was not yet lost. Italy, meanwhile, had luck on their side but they had announced they were a fine side.

At Rosario, **Tunisia** made their World Cup debut against **Mexico**. The Mexicans, young and inexperienced, were largely unimpressive but nevertheless they took the lead on the stroke of half-time. When Antonio de la Torre's cross from the left struck the hand of defender Amor Jebali, the referee had no choice but to award a penalty which skipper Arturo Vazquez Ayala converted for a 1-0 lead at the break. However, the North Africans returned a different side. Keeping things tight at the back, they poured forward, their midfield cleverly holding the ball up to play in their runners from behind. Ten minutes after the break they were deservedly level when Mohamed Ben Rehaiem Agrebi crossed from the right and defender Ali Kaabi's low shot from the edge of the area somehow trickled into the corner. Buoyed by their goal, the Africans scented blood and burst forward in the closing stages. Mexico could not hold them. First, the exceptional playmaker Tarak Dhiab played Nejib Ghommidh through to slot past keeper Jose Reyes before victory was confirmed three minutes from time after Ghommidh this time picked out the run of right-back Mokhtar Dhouib who smashed in a powerful effort off the underside of the bar. Tunisia, in their first World Cup match, had won gloriously, while Mexico had been exposed for their lack of experience.

That evening, at River Plate's Monumental stadium, hosts **Argentina** got their own World Cup adventure underway against **Hungary**, on paper the weakest side in Group One. However, the noisy, packed stadium was silenced after just ten minutes as Karoly Csapo followed up after Sandor Zombori's shot was blocked to fire in the opener. Nevertheless, the hosts quickly found a response, Sandor Gujdar unable to hold Mario Kempes' free-kick and Leopoldo Luque was on hand to poke in the rebound. The second half was spoiled by horrifically negative play from both teams, who sought to stop their opponents with consistent and violent fouling, with Hungary striker Andras Torocsik dealt with particularly brutally. Then, with seven minutes remaining, Argentina managed a scarcely deserved late winner, Gujdar coming out smartly to clear a building attack but the loose ball squirming to substitute winger Daniel Bertoni, who made no mistake. This heart-breaker was all too much for Torocsik, who meted out his own justice on Americo Gallego and was promptly dismissed. His team mate Tibor Nyilasi followed him barely a minute later for barging left-back Alberto Tarantini to the ground. Argentina had their all-important opening win but they had been somewhat fortunate, while Hungary had received a double-blow: they had lost and would have to play their next match against Italy without their two best players, both of whom would be suspended.

In the capital the following day, **Spain**, with the support of the neutrals of the crowd, took on **Austria** in Group Three. The Spanish were the favourites but no-one had told their opponents, who started with a bang in the opening exchanges. Centre-back Bruno Pezzey thumped the ball out of defence and found Walter Schachner racing down the right wing. The forward burst on, beat the left-back and smashed past Miguel Angel in the Spanish goal from a tight angle for a sublime opener. However, the Spanish were level at half-time, striker Dani on target to the delight of the home crowd. Nevertheless, the promptings of the exceptional Herbert Prohaska proved a constant thorn in the side of the Iberians and with 15 minutes to play they fell behind again thanks to an opportunistic finish from goal poacher Hans Krankl. Spain had suffered a major blow while Austria had announced they were a fine side themselves.

At the same time, their Group rivals **Brazil** and **Sweden** met in Mar del Plata. The Brazilians quickly laid siege to the Swedish goal but were guilty of profligate finishing on several occasions. The Scandinavians made them pay with their first real attack, veteran playmaker Bo Larsson supplying a glorious first-time through-ball for Thomas Sjoberg to slot beyond Emerson Leao. Stunned, Brazil could have fallen further behind minutes later but were fortunate to see Lennart Larsson's header go over via the crossbar with Leao hopelessly beaten. Indeed, the South Americans went in at half-time level thanks to an opportunistic finish from young striker Reinaldo, seizing on a defensive slip to convert Cerezo's hopeful punt forwards. The second period saw presentable opportunities for both teams but the game's greatest drama was saved for the death.

Only at the World Cup

Brazil's match with Sweden ended in great controversy when Welsh referee Clive Thomas disallowed a late Brazilian winner because he had blown the final whistle as Zico's header flew into the back of the net! Brazil were so furious they lodged an official protest, claiming bias, but this was rejected.

With the match entering injury time, Nelinho swung in a corner which Zico powerfully headed home but Brazilian joy soon turned to fury as it became clear that Welsh referee Clive Thomas had blown for full-time as the ball flew in and the goal would not stand. The players argued furiously but Thomas refused to listen, marching briskly from the field leaving a furious team in his wake.

Further afield in Cordoba, the much-fancied **Scotland** side sought to open their tournament with victory over **Peru**'s veterans. The thousands of travelling Scots expected an easy win and when Ramon Quiroga failed to hold onto a shot and Joe Jordan tapped in the rebound just 14 minutes in it seemed that would be what would transpire. Peru, and their outstanding midfielder and inspiration Teofilo Cubillas in particular, had other ideas, however. They started to worry their more illustrious opponents with pace, tricky running and gorgeous link-up play. Inevitably, they equalised before the break, a slick move finishing with midfielder Cesar Cueto breaking clear and slotting past Alan Rough. Scotland sought a response in the second half and got the perfect opportunity when they won a penalty for a clumsy challenge on Bruce Rioch. However, midfielder Don Masson saw his effort kept out by Quiroga's dive and the Scots had wasted a golden opportunity to get back in front. They were soon made to pay. Another quick Peruvian attack saw Cueto burst forward and find Cubillas. Peru's talisman stepped forward and unleashed an unstoppable swerving rocket from 25 yards which gave Rough no chance. Five minutes later it got even worse for the Scots when Peru won a free-kick in almost exactly the same spot from where Cubillas had just scored. Predictably, the same player charged up and fired home another thunderbolt which Rough was unable to keep out, despite getting a hand to it. Scotland, who had arrived at the tournament expecting to carry away the trophy, had been given a massive reality check, while Peru had shown they were still a dangerous side.

> **Only at the World Cup**
>
> If the Scots thought it couldn't get any worse after their humiliating loss to Peru they were wrong. Left winger Willie Johnston failed a drug test in the aftermath of the game and was expelled from the cup.

Meanwhile, further west at the Estadio Ciudad de Mendoza, the smallest of the finals' six venues, **Holland** wrapped up a fairly comfortable victory over debutants **Iran**. Perhaps it could have been so different had Iran striker Hossain Faraki connected with a cross from just two yards out with Dutch keeper Jan Jongbloed stranded but as it was, for all Iran's attractive play, they could not match the Orangemen for quality. In the absence of Johan Cruyff, Rob Rensenbrink took it upon himself to show his worth as a player, notching up a hat-trick. First he converted a penalty five minutes before half-time, then he headed in Rene Van de Kerkhof's cross on the hour before finally blasting his second penalty of the game into the top corner with some ten minutes left on the clock. Holland had the two points they desired but Iran had been anything but disgraced in their debut World Cup match.

Group Stage – Second series

Hungary, now shorn of their primary attacking threats Nyilasi and Torocsik, faced the formidable prospect of getting a result against the might of **Italy** to remain in the tournament. Predictably, this task proved beyond them, the Italians ruthlessly exposing them at the back in another impressive performance. Hungarian hopes had effectively been extinguished by half-time as strikers Paolo Rossi and Roberto Bettega both scored, the latter after being put through by exceptional playmaker Franco Causio. On the hour, Romeo Benetti was in the right place to make sure of it after the Hungarian defence was again unable to fight the fires bursting out all around. At least a late penalty from substitute Andras Toth gave them some small consolation.

Back in Group Two, **Tunisia** sought to build on their fantastic victory against Mexico with another positive result against their next opponents, **Poland**, in Rosario. The Europeans started strongly enough, Jerzy Gorgon heading down for Wlodzimierz Lubanski to slot home only for the linesman to flag for offside. However, the Poles were ahead before half-time, Grzegorz Lato playing the ball to Lubanski and racing into the area to convert his return courtesy of a horrendous missed kick by Tunisia left-back Ali Kaabi. Poland should have stretched their lead in the second period but they were unimpressive and were almost made to pay by a late surge from the Carthage Eagles in the final quarter. With the miniscule crowd firmly behind them, the Africans poured forward, captain Temime Lahzami crashing an effort off the underside of the bar and Mohamed Ben Rehaiem Agrebi twice coming desperately close to equalising. The North African debutants, despite the narrow defeat, were proving a revelation at the finals and Poland could count themselves hugely fortunate to have won the game.

Meanwhile, reigning champions **West Germany** emphatically found their form against **Mexico**, putting the Central Americans to the sword in Cordoba. The Mexicans started brightly but as soon as striker Dieter Muller received the ball on the edge of the area, slipped his marker and expertly found the far corner of the net 15 minutes in it all went rapidly downhill for the Latin side. Quarter of an hour later a superb run from midfield from Heinz Flohe finished with the perfect through-ball for Hansi Muller to make it two and after that it was one-way traffic. A Mexican free-kick went awry and allowed new young star Karl-Heinz Rummenigge to ride through the challenges, burst into the box and poke the ball past the keeper for an exceptional solo goal and before half-time it was four as the Germans showed Mexico how to take a free-kick; Rainer Bonhof laid the ball off for Flohe to blast in from 30 yards and it was all over for Mexico. When Klaus Fischer's cross was laid back by Hansi Muller and rifled in by Rummenigge after 73 minutes it prompted another burst of German attacks. Fischer and Rummenigge both wasted great openings, Flohe struck both posts before the midfielder finally crowned his great performance with a sixth goal, racing forward from halfway, side-stepping a defender and cracking a thunderous effort into the top corner. Mexico had been humiliated by the German juggernaut and there was no doubt that the 6-0 scoreline hugely flattered the outclassed Central Americans.

> ## Only at the World Cup
>
> Mexico showed in their game with the Germans that even winning a free-kick deep in your opponent's half can be dangerous! An attempt at an elaborate set piece ended in farce as Guillermo Mendizabal failed to anticipate that the ball was intended for him, allowing Rummenigge to steal in and run almost the whole length of the field to score!

> ## Only at the World Cup
>
> Mexico may have been beaten savagely by Germany but it would have been worse but for Heinz Flohe's bad luck with a second-half shot. The midfielder saw his effort thud into the right-hand post, cannon back across the face, strike the left-hand post, bounce out and hit a defender before it was eventually gathered by the bemused goalkeeper!

Argentina and **France** met in the evening chill at Buenos Aires and the hordes of home fans hoped for a more convincing performance than the narrow and fortunate win over Hungary. However, the hosts were largely outplayed by France before winning a penalty against Marius Tresor on the stroke of half-time that was dubious at best. Captain Daniel Passarella converted and France had it all to do. However, they did not shirk their task and when Michel Platini fired in after a goalmouth scramble they were back in the game. Platini was starting to pull the strings and the whole of Argentina had their hearts in their mouths when he played Didier Six clean through on

Only at the World Cup

France keeper Jean-Paul Bertrand-Demanes suffered a sickening injury against Argentina. In tipping over a lob he fell into his goal post head first, damaging his spine and ending his international career.

goal, only for the forward to guide his effort agonisingly wide. Then, with Argentina seemingly on the ropes, the hosts somehow found a late winner of the highest quality. Osvaldo Ardiles played the ball into the feet of Leopoldo Luque some 25 yards from goal; in a flash the striker flicked the ball up and crashed an unstoppable volley into the corner on the turn. The home country celebrated this fabulous winner wildly but in truth they had again been lucky to win and France, like Hungary, could feel aggrieved about some of the officiating.

In Group Three, two uninspired games took place. At Mar del Plata, **Brazil** slumped to their second successive bore draw, with their opponents **Spain** just as unimpressive as they had been against Austria. Neither side could fashion any decent openings and the game quickly petered out into a pitiful affair bereft of excitement and invention which left both sides with plenty of work to do to reach the next stage.

Meanwhile in Buenos Aires, **Austria** recorded their second successive win of the group but hardly in the most emphatic fashion against **Sweden**. Hans Krankl scored the only goal of the game from the penalty spot just before half-time and from then on the Austrians dominated without really trying to stretch their lead. They had qualified for the second round and impressed while the Swedes had lacked any real invention and would need to beat Spain in their final game to have any hopes of qualifying along with their conquerors.

Group Four would also do little to enhance what had otherwise to this point been a tournament full of quality football, throwing up two lifeless and unexciting draws. In Mendoza, **Holland** showed remarkably little ambition and seemed perfectly happy to draw 0-0 with **Peru**. Indeed, it was the South Americans who looked the more likely scorers throughout the game, striker Guillermo La Rosa coming closest with a shot that skimmed the top of the bar.

Scotland and **Iran**, defeated in their opening games, desperately needed to win and most expected the Scots to do so easily, despite the absence of disgraced winger Willie Johnston. It started well enough for them as they went ahead before the break thanks to a shockingly inept own goal from defender Andranik Eskandarian, who in attempting to clear the ball behind only sliced it straight into the back of the net from the edge of the area. However, the Scots were given a mighty shock on the hour when Iraj Danaifar picked up the ball after a half-clearance, skinned Archie Gemmill on the right of the area and beat Alan Rough from a tight angle for an improbable equaliser. Scotland could find no answer in the closing stages and, for all their talk of winning the tournament, they had been utterly humiliated in their first two games and had next to no chance of reaching the second round.

Group Stage – Third series

Only at the World Cup

France's match with Hungary was almost postponed because the two sides arrived with the same colour kit! In the end, the French were forced to wear the strip of local team Atletico Kimberley.

Both already eliminated, **France** and **Hungary** met in a game played for nothing but pride at Mar del Plata. A colour clash between the sides led to the start being delayed while replacement shirts were found from a local club before the two teams eventually took to the field, with the French kitted out in unfamiliar green and white stripes. With the pressure off, a thrilling first half followed as both teams attacked relentlessly. France drew first blood when defender Christian Lopez thumped a glorious

30-yard drive into the top corner and the lead was soon doubled after Marc Berdoll's persistence up front paid off as he weaved his way past defenders into a shooting position and tucked the ball into the far corner. However, Hungary came storming back with a wonder goal of their own, Sandor Zombori playing a one-two with Tibor Nyilasi before chipping Dominique Dropsy spectacularly. Still, there was another goal before half-time, Dominique Rocheteau in the right place to turn home Olivier Rouyer's lay-off. Sadly, the second half was unable to match the first for thrills but still attacking football dominated and the French at least had a consolation win to celebrate before the long flight home.

In Cordoba in Group Two, **West Germany** sought to carry the form of their thrashing of Mexico into their encounter with **Tunisia**. Instead, they displayed all the nerves of their error-strewn opener and were quite unable to contain the pace, invention and bravery of the North Africans. They failed to sparkle as an attacking force and several times survived Tunisia's increasingly confident attacks only by the skin of their teeth. The world champions were hugely fortunate to hold onto their 0-0 draw to the finish, which was just enough to see them through to the second round at the expense of Tunisia. However, the Africans had been exceptional throughout the tournament and had greatly enhanced both their own reputation and that of football on their continent.

Meanwhile at Rosario, **Poland** took advantage of the Germans' slip-up to take top spot in the group with an easy victory over **Mexico**. The Mexicans at least showed some improvement from their first two games but they were still comprehensively beaten and fell behind before half-time thanks to a visionary pass from Kazimierz Deyna to pick out the run of Grzegorz Lato, whose cross was coolly converted by young Zbigniew Boniek. The Mexicans briefly equalised somewhat fortuitously in the second period when Ignacio Flores' cross struck Victor Rangel and flew in but the lead lasted just four minutes before Deyna met Andrzej Iwan's lay-off with a smash into the roof of the net. Before the end, Boniek had added yet another stunning long-range strike to a tournament already overflowing with them, swerving an outrageous effort into the top corner from 30 yards. The Poles had again shown their quality.

Back in Buenos Aires, **Argentina** and **Italy** did battle for top spot in Group One, both already assured of reaching the second phase. With a noisy and passionate crowd, predictably it was the hosts who did most of the running but their attacks floundered on the rock of the Italian defence. The Europeans, an exceptional side, stole a deserved winner in the second half, Paolo Rossi finding his strike partner Roberto Bettega to slot past Ubaldo Fillol into the corner. Argentina had been proven vulnerable and they paid a high price for their defeat, as it deprived them of playing in front of their hordes of fans in the capital in the second round. Italy, meanwhile, had given a clear demonstration of their title credentials with their perfect and hugely impressive record in so tough a group.

Brazil faced **Austria** knowing that in all likelihood they would need to beat opponents who had so far impressed in the competition to reach the next phase. This they achieved but not without a great deal of difficulty. They scored in the first half when Gil's cross from deep found Roberto Dinamite and the talented striker made no mistake with his finish. However, in the second period the South Americans were forced to cling on as the Austrians again underlined their ability. Goalkeeper Emerson Leao was a busy man but in the end he proved equal to what his opponents threw at him. Brazil may not have impressed but crucially they had reached the next stage.

As this contest was taking place, **Spain** and **Sweden** were frantically clinging to their slim hopes of progress from the same group. Both sides had been poor so far in the tournament but in Buenos Aires, with the crowd firmly behind them, Spain found their form and victory thanks to Juan Manuel Asensi's goal from Juanito's pass. However, at the end the news of Brazil's victory rendered their efforts academic. Heartbroken, they would head home together with Sweden.

Scotland went into their final Group Four game in Mendoza facing a mountainous task to qualify: they would have to beat mighty

> ### Stat Attack
>
> Rensenbrink's goal against Scotland was the 1,000th in World Cup history.

Holland by three goals. This seemed next to impossible, especially given the Scots' atrocious performances in their first two games. However, undeniably talented, Scotland came out for the match a different side and tore into the 1974 runners-up from the off, Joe Jordan heading against the bar, Bruce Rioch striking the post and Kenny Dalglish seeing an effort harshly ruled out for an alleged foul. Then, utterly against the run of play, the Dutch won a penalty against Stuart Kennedy which Rob Rensenbrink converted. However, far from wallowing in self-pity, the Scots continued their positive, attractive play and this bore dividends when Jordan headed down and Dalglish slotted past Jan Jongbloed. Minutes after the break the British side were deservedly in front when they won a penalty of their own, which midfielder Archie Gemmill struck firmly into the corner. The best was yet to come, however, as Gemmill came up with one of the most astonishing individual goals at any World Cup. Picking the ball up out wide on the right of the edge of the area, the diminutive Scot dropped his shoulder and weaved his way through the despairing challenges of three Dutch defenders before cheekily lobbing Jongbloed. The Tartan Army went wild and Scotland needed just one more goal to seal shock qualification. Sadly for the brave Scots, the game's final goal arrived at the other end, Johnny Rep smashing a dipping effort into the top corner from 25 yards, but nothing could take the gloss off a famous and well-deserved victory. Still, if only the Scots had played with the same freedom, ability and heart in their first two games they could have been real contenders in the tournament.

> ### Only at the World Cup
>
> Gemmill's famous second goal made an appearance in the cult movie Trainspotting, where it is playing in the background while a couple are having sex. Ewan McGregor's character then exclaims: "I haven't felt that good since Archie Gemmill scored against Holland in 1978!"

Holland's surprise defeat meant **Peru** took top spot in Group Four courtesy of their 4-1 win over **Iran**. Just two minutes in, Jose Velasquez headed in Juan Jose Munante's corner for 1-0. Teofilo Cubillas stretched Peru's lead from the penalty spot before three minutes later the same player's majestic dribble was eventually halted illegally in the area, allowing him to double his tally with another penalty. Iran pulled a goal back before half-time when Peru failed to clear a left-wing cross, allowing the dangerous Hassan Rowshan to slot in from the edge of the area. Nevertheless, the day belonged to Peru and their star Cubillas, who completed a thoroughly deserved hat-trick after collecting the ball with his back to goal, leaving two defenders standing before comfortably beating keeper Nasser Hejazi.

> ### Stat Attack
>
> Teofilo Cubillas' hat-trick against Iran made him the first player to score five goals in each of two different World Cups, a record which only Miroslav Klose has emulated. Cubillas is also the highest scoring midfielder in the competition's history, with ten goals.

First Round results

Group 1

Italy 2-1 France
02/06/78 – Mar del Plata (Jose Maria Minella)
Italy: Zoff (c), Gentile, Bellugi, Scirea, Cabrini, Benetti, Tardelli, Antognoni (Zaccarelli), Causio, Rossi, Bettega
Goals: Rossi 29, Zaccarelli 52
France: Bertrand-Demanes, Janvion, Rio, Tresor (c), Bossis, Guillou, Michel, Platini, Dalger, Lacombe (Berdoll), Six (Rouyer)
Goals: Lacombe 1
Referee: Rainea (Romania)

Argentina 2-1 Hungary
02/06/78 – Buenos Aires (Monumental)
Argentina: Fillol, Olguin, L Galvan, Passarella (c), Tarantini, Ardiles, Gallego, Valencia (Alonso), Houseman (Bertoni), Luque, Kempes
Goals: Luque 15, Bertoni 83
Hungary: Gujdar, Torok (Martos), Kereki (c), Kocsis, J Toth, Nyilasi, Zombori, Pinter, Csapo, Torocsik, Nagy
Goals: Csapo 10
Sent off: Torocsik 88, Nyilasi 89
Referee: Garrido (Portugal)

Italy 3-1 Hungary
06/06/78 – Mar del Plata (Jose Maria Minella)
Italy: Zoff (c), Gentile, Bellugi, Scirea, Cabrini (Cuccureddu), Benetti, Tardelli, Antognoni, Causio, Rossi, Bettega (Graziani)
Goals: Rossi 34, Bettega 36, Benetti 60
Hungary: Meszaros, Martos, Kereki (c), Kocsis, J Toth, Zombori, Pinter, Csapo, Pusztai, Fazekas (Halasz), Nagy (A Toth)
Goals: A Toth pen 81
Referee: Barreto (Uruguay)

Argentina 2-1 France
06/06/78 – Buenos Aires (Monumental)
Argentina: Fillol, Olguin, L Galvan, Passarella (c), Tarantini, Ardiles, Gallego, Valencia (Alonso) (Ortiz), Houseman, Luque, Kempes
Goals: Passarella pen 45, Luque 73
France: Bertrand-Demanes (Baratelli), Battiston, Lopez, Tresor (c), Bossis, Bathenay, Michel, Platini, Rocheteau, Lacombe, Six
Goals: Platini 60
Referee: Dubach (Switzerland)

France 3-1 Hungary

10/06/78 – Mar del Plata (Jose Maria Minella)

France: Dropsy, Janvion, Lopez, Tresor (c), Bracci, Bathenay, Petit, Papi (Platini), Rocheteau (Six), Berdoll, Rouyer

Goals: Lopez 22, Berdoll 37, Rocheteau 42

Hungary: Gujdar, Martos, Kereki (c), Balint, J Toth, Nyilasi, Zombori, Pinter, Pusztai, Torocsik, Nagy (Csapo)

Goals: Zombori 41

Referee: Coelho (Brazil)

Italy 1-0 Argentina

10/06/78 – Buenos Aires (Monumental)

Italy: Zoff (c), Gentile, Bellugi (Cuccureddu), Scirea, Cabrini, Benetti, Tardelli, Antognoni (Zaccarelli), Causio, Rossi, Bettega

Goals: Bettega 67

Argentina: Fillol, Olguin, L Galvan, Passarella (c), Tarantini, Ardiles, Gallego, Valencia, Bertoni, Kempes, Ortiz (Houseman)

Referee: Klein (Israel)

	Pld	W	D	L	GF	GA	Pts
Italy	3	3	0	0	6	2	6
Argentina	3	2	0	1	4	3	4
France	3	1	0	2	5	5	2
Hungary	3	0	0	3	3	8	0

Italy and Argentina qualified for second round.

Group 2

West Germany 0-0 Poland

01/06/78 – Buenos Aires (Monumental)

West Germany: Maier, Vogts (c), Russmann, Zimmermann, Kaltz, Bonhof, Beer, Flohe, H Muller, Abramczik, Fischer

Poland: Tomaszewski, Szymanowski, Gorgon, Zmuda, Maculewicz, Nawalka, Deyna (c), Masztaler (Kasperczak), Lato, Lubanski (Boniek), Szarmach

Referee: Coerezza (Argentina)

Tunisia 3-1 Mexico

02/06/78 – Rosario (Gigante de Arroyito)

Tunisia: Naili, Dhouib, Labidi Jendoubi, Jebali, Kaabi, Ghommidh, Ben Rehaiem Agrebi, Dhiab, Temime (c) (Labidi), Akid, Ben Aziza (Karoui)

Goals: Kaabi 55, Ghommidh 79, Dhouib 87

Mexico: Reyes, Martinez, Tena, Ramos, Vazquez Ayala (c), de la Torre, Cuellar, Mendizabal (Lugo), Isiordia, Rangel, Sanchez

Goals: Vazquez Ayala pen 45

Referee: Gordon (Scotland)

Poland 1-0 Tunisia

06/06/78 – Rosario (Gigante de Arroyito)

Poland: Tomaszewski, Szymanowski, Gorgon, Zmuda, Maculewicz, Nawalka, Deyna (c), Kasperczak, Lato, Lubanski (Boniek), Szarmach (Iwan)

Goals: Lato 43

Tunisia: Naili, Dhouib, Labidi Jendoubi, Jebali, Kaabi, Ghommidh, Gasmi, Ben Rehaiem Agrebi, Dhiab, Temime (c), Akid

Referee: Martinez (Spain)

West Germany 6-0 Mexico

06/06/78 – Cordoba (Estadio Cordoba)

West Germany: Maier, Vogts (c), Russmann, Dietz, Kaltz, Bonhof, Flohe, H Muller, Rummenigge, Fischer, D Muller

Goals: D Muller 15, H Muller 30, Rummenigge 38, 73, Flohe 44, 89

Mexico: Reyes (Soto), Martinez, Tena, Ramos, Vazquez Ayala (c), de la Torre, Cuellar, Mendizabal, Lopez Zarza (Lugo), Rangel, Sanchez

Referee: Bouzo (Syria)

West Germany 0-0 Tunisia

10/06/78 – Cordoba (Estadio Cordoba)

West Germany: Maier, Vogts (c), Russmann, Dietz, Kaltz, Bonhof, Flohe, H Muller, Rummenigge, Fischer, D Muller

Tunisia: Naili, Dhouib, Labidi Jendoubi, Jebali, Kaabi, Ghommidh, Gasmi, Ben Rehaiem Agrebi, Dhiab, Temime (c), Akid (Ben Aziza)

Referee: Orosco (Peru)

Poland 3-1 Mexico

10/06/78 – Rosario (Gigante de Arroyito)

Poland: Tomaszewski, Szymanowski, Gorgon, Zmuda, Rudy (Maculewicz), Kasperczak, Deyna (c), Masztaler, Boniek, Lato, Iwan (Lubanski)

Goals: Boniek 43, 84, Deyna 56

Mexico: Soto, Gomez, Cisneros, Flores, Vazquez Ayala (c), de la Torre, Cuellar, Cardenas (Mendizabal), Ortega, Rangel, Sanchez

Goals: Rangel 52

Referee: Namdar (Iran)

	Pld	W	D	L	GF	GA	Pts
Poland	3	2	1	0	4	1	5
West Germany	3	1	2	0	6	0	4
Tunisia	3	1	1	1	3	2	3
Mexico	3	0	0	3	2	12	0

Poland and West Germany qualified for second round.

Group 3

Austria 2-1 Spain
03/06/78 – Buenos Aires (Jose Amalfitani)
Austria: Koncilia, Sara (c), Pezzey, Obermayer, Breitenberger, Hickersberger (Weber), Prohaska, Jara, Schachner (Pirkner), Krankl, Kreuz
Goals: Schachner 9, Krankl 76
Spain: Miguel Angel, Marcelino, Migueli, Pirri (c), de la Cruz, San Jose, Asensi, Cardenosa (Leal), Rexach (Quini), Dani, Ruben Cano
Goals: Dani 21
Referee: Palotai (Hungary)

Brazil 1-1 Sweden
03/06/78 – Mar del Plata (Jose Maria Minella)
Brazil: Leao, Toninho, Amaral, Oscar, Edinho, Cerezo (Dirceu), Batista, Zico, Gil (Nelinho), Reinaldo, Rivelino (c)
Goals: Reinaldo 45
Sweden: Hellstrom, Borg, Roy Andersson, Nordqvist (c), Erlandsson, L Larsson (Edstrom), Tapper, Linderoth, B Larsson, Sjoberg, Wendt
Goals: Sjoberg 37
Referee: Thomas (Wales)

Brazil 0-0 Spain
07/06/78 – Mar del Plata (Jose Maria Minella)
Brazil: Leao (c), Toninho, Amaral, Oscar, Edinho, Nelinho (Gil), Cerezo, Batista, Dirceu, Zico (Mendonca), Reinaldo
Spain: Miguel Angel, Marcelino, Migueli (Biosca), Uria (Guzman), Olmo, San Jose, Asensi (c), Cardenosa, Leal, Juanito, Santillana
Referee: Gonella (Italy)

Austria 1-0 Sweden
07/06/78 – Buenos Aires (Jose Amalfitani)
Austria: Koncilia, Sara (c), Pezzey, Obermayer, Breitenberger, Hickersberger, Prohaska, Krieger (Weber), Jara, Krankl, Kreuz
Goals: Krankl pen 42
Sweden: Hellstrom, Borg, Roy Andersson, Nordqvist (c), Erlandsson, L Larsson, Tapper (Torstensson), Linderoth (Edstrom), B Larsson, Sjoberg, Wendt
Referee: Corver (Holland)

Brazil 1-0 Austria
11/06/78 – Mar del Plata (Jose Maria Minella)
Brazil: Leao (c), Toninho, Amaral, Oscar, Rodrigues Neto, Cerezo (Chicao), Batista, Dirceu, Gil, Mendonca (Zico), Roberto Dinamite
Goals: Roberto Dinamite 40
Austria: Koncilia, Sara (c), Pezzey, Obermayer, Breitenberger, Hickersberger (Weber), Prohaska, Krieger (Happich), Jara, Krankl, Kreuz
Referee: Wurtz (France)

Spain 1-0 Sweden

11/06/78 – Buenos Aires (Jose Amalfitani)

Spain: Miguel Angel, Marcelino, Biosca, Uria, Olmo (Pirri), San Jose, Asensi (c), Cardenosa, Leal, Juanito, Santillana

Goals: Asensi 75

Sweden: Hellstrom, Borg, Roy Andersson, Nordqvist (c), Erlandsson, L Larsson, Nordin, B Larsson, Nilsson, Sjoberg (Linderoth), Edstrom (Wendt)

Referee: Biwersi (West Germany)

	Pld	W	D	L	GF	GA	Pts
Austria	3	2	0	1	3	2	4
Brazil	3	1	2	0	2	1	4
Spain	3	1	1	1	2	2	3
Sweden	3	0	1	2	1	3	1

Austria and Brazil qualified for second round.

Group 4

Peru 3-1 Scotland

03/06/78 – Cordoba (Estadio Cordoba)

Peru: Quiroga, Duarte, Chumpitaz (c), Diaz, Manzo, Cueto (P Rojas), Velasquez, Cubillas, Munante, La Rosa (Sotil), Oblitas

Goals: Cueto 43, Cubillas 72, 77

Scotland: Rough, Kennedy (c), Burns, Buchan, Forsyth, Rioch (Gemmill), Masson (Macari), Hartford, Dalglish, Jordan, Johnston

Goals: Jordan 14

Referee: Eriksson (Sweden)

Holland 3-0 Iran

03/06/78 – Mendoza (Ciudad de Mendoza)

Holland: Jongbloed, Suurbier, Krol (c), Rijsbergen, Jansen, Neeskens, Haan, W Van de Kerkhof, R Van de Kerkhof (Nanninga), Rep, Rensenbrink

Goals: Rensenbrink pen 40, 62, pen 79

Iran: Hejazi, Nazari, Kazerani, Eskandarian, Abdollahi, Parvin (c), Ghasempour, Sadeghi, Nayebagha, Jahani, Faraki (Rowshan)

Referee: Archundia (Mexico)

Holland 0-0 Peru

07/06/78 – Mendoza (Ciudad de Mendoza)

Holland: Jongbloed, Suurbier, Krol (c), Poortvliet, Rijsbergen, Jansen, Neeskens (Nanninga), Haan, W Van de Kerkhof, R Van de Kerkhof (Rep), Rensenbrink

Peru: Quiroga, Duarte, Chumpitaz (c), Diaz, Manzo, Cueto, Velasquez, Cubillas, Munante, La Rosa (Sotil), Oblitas

Referee: Prokop (East Germany)

Scotland 1-1 Iran
07/06/78 – Cordoba (Estadio Cordoba)
Scotland: Rough, Jardine, Burns, Buchan (Forsyth), Donachie, Gemmill (c), Macari, Hartford, Dalglish (Harper), Jordan, Robertson
Goals: Eskandarian (og) 43
Iran: Hejazi, Nazari, Kazerani, Eskandarian, Abdollahi, Parvin (c), Ghasempour, Sadeghi, Danaifar (Nayebagha), Jahani, Faraki (Rowshan)
Goals: Danaifar 60
Referee: N'Diaye (Senegal)

Scotland 3-2 Holland
11/06/78 – Mendoza (Ciudad de Mendoza)
Scotland: Rough, Kennedy (c), Buchan, Forsyth, Donachie, Gemmill, Rioch, Souness, Hartford, Dalglish, Jordan
Goals: Dalglish 44, Gemmill pen 47, 68
Holland: Jongbloed, Suurbier, Krol (c), Poortvliet, Rijsbergen (Wildschut), Jansen, Neeskens (Boskamp), W Van de Kerkhof, R Van de Kerkhof, Rep, Rensenbrink
Goals: Rensenbrink pen 34, Rep 71
Referee: Linemayr (Austria)

Peru 4-1 Iran
11/06/78 – Cordoba (Estadio Cordoba)
Peru: Quiroga, Duarte, Chumpitaz (c), Diaz, Manzo (Leguia), Cueto, Velasquez, Cubillas, Munante, La Rosa (Sotil), Oblitas
Goals: Velasquez 2, Cubillas pen 36, pen 39, 79
Iran: Hejazi, Nazari, Kazerani, Allahverdi, Abdollahi, Parvin (c), Ghasempour, Sadeghi, Danaifar, Rowshan (Fariba), Faraki (Jahani)
Goals: Rowshan 41
Referee: Jarguz (Poland)

	Pld	W	D	L	GF	GA	Pts
Peru	3	2	1	0	7	2	5
Holland	3	1	1	1	5	3	3
Scotland	3	1	1	1	5	6	3
Iran	3	0	1	2	2	8	1

Peru and Holland qualified for second round.

Second Round Group Draw

Group A

Italy (Winner Group One)
West Germany (Runner-up Group Two)
Austria (Winner Group Three)
Holland (Runner-up Group Four)

Group B

Argentina (Runner-up Group One)
Poland (Winner Group Two)
Brazil (Runner-up Group Three)
Peru (Winner Group Four)

Second Round – First series

The first game of the second round was a mouth-watering clash in the capital between European powerhouses **West Germany**, the reigning champions, and **Italy**, many people's favourites for the title on the basis of their exceptional first-round performances. The last World Cup encounter between the two had been the incredible "Game of the Century" in the 1970 semi-final and many hoped for a repeat. As it was the game provided gripping drama from start to finish, even if it was unable to quite hit the heights hoped. The Italian rearguard was more troubled than it had been at any stage of the first round but Dino Zoff held firm in goal, while Paolo Rossi and Roberto Bettega looked to pounce on any opportunity at the other end. However, Germany keeper Sepp Maier was in just as imperious form as his opposite number and on the rare occasions he was beaten his team mates where there to help, Manfred Kaltz acrobatically clearing off the line. The best chance of the game saw Italy left-back Antonio Cabrini strike the post but in the end 0-0 would have to do. The scoreline, however, gave no reflection at all of the great excitement and drama the encounter had provided.

Holland's coach Ernst Happel reacted to defeat at the hands of Scotland by making several changes to his starting line-up and his new look side arrived in Cordoba firing on all cylinders to blow away the challenge of his homeland **Austria**. The Dutch took an early lead when Arie Haan's floated free-kick was headed in by one of the replacements, defender Ernie Brandts. Austria sought a response but were caught out on the break and conceded a penalty converted by Rob Rensenbrink. Rensenbrink was a constant menace to his opponents and a

> **Stat Attack**
>
> Rob Rensenbrink's goal against Austria was his fifth of the tournament, his fourth from the spot.

minute later he burst forward, stepped past a defender's challenge, drew keeper Friedrich Koncilia off his line and squared for Johnny Rep to score. Holland's relentless assault continued into the second half, Rensenbrink again putting it on a plate for Rep to double his personal tally. Austria had not played poorly by any means but the Dutch had ruthlessly punished their mistakes and caught them on the break time and again. The Austrians were certainly deserving of getting on the scoresheet and they at least achieved this ten minutes before the end, sweeper Erich Obermayer lifting the ball over new keeper Piet Schrijvers. Austria briefly threatened a late revival, a stinging long range drive from Gerhard Breitenberger being superbly tipped round the post by Schrijvers. However, the game's final goal arrived at the other end, Rensenbrink crowning his fabulous individual performance with his third assist of the game, superbly picking out Willy Van de Kerkhof to thump home goal number five. Holland had shown that even without Cruyff they were serious contenders for the title.

Group B kicked off in Mendoza with an all-South American affair between **Peru** and **Brazil**. It was the Peruvians who started the stronger, catching Brazil cold early on and unlucky not to take an early lead, with Emerson Leao in goal keeping his side level. Then, from what was almost Brazil's first attack, the Selecao won a free-kick 25 yards from goal. Midfielder Dirceu stepped up and produced the perfect shot, swerving away outrageously into the top far corner, rendering it utterly unsaveable. Stunned, Peru suffered a further and wholly preventable blow soon after: Dirceu's shot from the edge of the area lacked any real power but keeper Ramon Quiroga somehow let it squirm through his grasp to trickle into the far corner. Quiroga sought to redeem his error with a series of impressive saves but the damage had been done and, when Jaime Duarte fouled Roberto Dinamite in the area in the second half, Zico tucked away the penalty to complete a comfortable win. Brazil were starting to find their form.

Rosario got its chance to welcome the home team **Argentina** that evening as they took on **Poland** in a match utterly bereft of sportsmanship. With foul play, rough tackling and cynical off-the-ball incidents throughout, it was at times a disgraceful spectacle. Argentina were still missing lead striker Leopoldo Luque due to the death of his brother four days earlier but in his absence youngster Mario Kempes was able to step out of his shadow. The Valencia man put the hosts ahead early on when he outpaced Antoni Szymanowski to head in Daniel Bertoni's cross from the left. The Poles were undeterred and poured forward, with Zbigniew Boniek a constant threat with his pace. However, the Argentinean defence soon resorted to scything down the youngster, disgracefully escaping punishment from the referee for their savage actions. Before the break Poland had a chance to get back into the game when they won a penalty after a home defender disgracefully blocked a shot on the line with a blatant and deliberate handball. However, Ubaldo Fillol saved Kazimierz Deyna's weak shot and Argentina maintained their lead. In the second period the Poles laid siege to their opponents' goal but couldn't find the equaliser they so richly deserved, Fillol performing heroics in tipping round a swinging Deyna free-kick. Instead it was the home side that doubled their tally, the superb Rene Houseman finding Kempes in the area once more and the forward shimmied past Henryk Maculewicz before shooting decisively beyond Jan Tomaszewski. Argentina had won but at times their play had been disgraceful.

Second Round – Second series

In Mendoza, **Poland** and **Peru** sought to bounce back from their opening defeats and stay in with a chance of making the final. It was the Poles, so unlucky to lose to Argentina, who dominated the game from start to finish. Secure at the back, Kazimierz Deyna and young Zbigniew Boniek pulled the

> ## Only at the World Cup
>
> Peru goalkeeper Ramon Quiroga lived up to his nickname of "El Loco" (the Crazy One) by being booked for a foul in his opponent's half against Poland, wrestling Grzegorz Lato to the ground as the winger attempted to break upfield!

strings in midfield, providing constant menace. It was a surprise that it took 65 minutes for the deadlock to finally be broken, Grzegorz Lato crossing for Andrzej Szarmach to head past Ramon Quiroga, but once it did arrive there never looked any prospect of the Europeans giving up their lead. Even Quiroga frequently bursting upfield to help his team mates was not enough to save Peru and they would go no further in the tournament.

In Group A **Italy** kept their seemingly unstoppable march to the final going with victory over **Austria** at the Estadio Monumental, eliminating the Austrians at the same time. Predatory striker Paolo Rossi pounced on hesitant defending early on to give the Italians a lead they never looked like surrendering. Austria remained positive but for all their attacking intent they never looked likely to breach the formidable Azzurri rearguard and in truth Italy would have won far more convincingly than 1-0 had they taken the second-half opportunities that fell their way on the break. Nevertheless, they still seemed a superb bet to take the trophy.

In a repeat of the 1974 World Cup final, **West Germany** and **Holland** met in Cordoba seeking a place in another final. Neither side was of quite the same quality as four years previously but they were still packed with world-class players and the match promised much. The Dutch were widely favoured but the Germans had been underdogs when they won that final and they took the lead after just three minutes when Rainer Bonhof's strongly-struck free-kick was tipped out by Schrijvers but Rudiger Abramczik stooped to head the rebound back past him. Still, the Dutch were undeterred and restored parity when Arie Haan let fly from 40 yards, the ball whistling past a stunned Sepp Maier and into the corner for a quite staggering goal. Holland, with Rob Rensenbrink exceptional, sensed victory but as they attacked they were caught cold by the Germans, Erich Beer crossing from the left and Dieter Muller expertly cushioning a header into the corner. Holland attacked relentlessly, twice hitting the woodwork, but as time ticked down it seemed as if it would not be their day. However, the Dutch were to find a late and deserved equaliser, Rene Van de Kerkhof receiving the ball on the edge of the area, side-stepping Bernard Dietz and curling the ball past Maier into the back of the net, despite Rolf Russmann attempting to clear the ball off the line with his arm. There was to be inevitable controversy before the end, however, as substitute Dick Nanninga was sent off just nine minutes after arriving on the field, dismissed farcically by Uruguayan referee Ramon Barreto for speaking to him in a language he did not understand!

That day's evening kick-off saw two other bitter rivals go head-to-head, this time the South American pair of **Brazil** and **Argentina**, who met in Rosario. The hosts' coach Menotti had responded to his side's unconvincing performances in the tournament with a reshuffle of his line-up: the return of striker Leopoldo Luque saw Mario Kempes drop back into midfield, taking the place of Daniel Valencia, while Oscar Ortiz replaced Rene Houseman on the wing. However, despite these changes, it was Brazil who dominated the game. They had several chances to take the lead but Ubaldo Fillol enjoyed a fine game between the sticks for the hosts. The match was spoiled for the most part with the aggression and cynicism the two sides treated each other with, with the home side particularly guilty of some shocking fouls and despicable play-acting. Despite such antics, however, neither team was able to break the deadlock as the game petered out into a 0-0 draw. The stalemate meant both sides could still harbour genuine ambitions of reaching the final.

Second Round – Third series

So to Cordoba and the last round of matches, where **West Germany** knew they would have to beat **Austria** to stand any chance of defending their trophy in the final. With a strong possibility that the qualifier from Group A would be decided on goal difference, the Germans sought to score as many as possible and they took an early lead when Dieter Muller picked out the run of Karl-Heinz Rummenigge, the young forward finishing easily. The Germans looked to be comfortably in control and in the hunt for more goals until just before the hour when a piece of fortune let their neighbours and rivals back into the game. An Austrian cross from the right wing seemed to pose little danger but skipper Berti Vogts, attempting to shepherd it back into the arms of keeper Sepp Maier, inadvertently flicked it beyond his grasp into the back of the net. Austria were improbably level and seven minutes later they took an even more unlikely lead. Eduard Krieger crossed from the left and striker Hans Krankl sublimely pulled the ball down out of the sky on his boot and unleashed a stunning volley past the shocked Maier. The Germans were behind but they showed their character to equalise almost immediately, Rainer Bonhof's right-wing free-kick headed in by Bernd Holzenbein. With time running out, it looked as if that might be it but no-one had told the indefatigable Krankl. Racing in from the left, the predatory striker weaved past the challenges of Vogts and Rolf Russmann before slipping the ball past the despairing Maier. At the end the Austrians wildly celebrated a rare victory over their more successful neighbours and they could take even further pride in that with it they had extinguished German hopes of defending their title.

Germany's defeat meant the winner of **Italy**'s clash with **Holland** in Buenos Aires would reach the final, with the Dutch needing just a draw thanks to their superior goal difference. Nevertheless, the Italians dominated from the start, showing defensive solidity and attacking intent. They took the lead after 18 minutes when Ernie Brandts, attempting to knock the ball away from the advancing Roberto Bettega, only succeeded in slotting it into the net himself. Worse still, in doing so Brandts collided with his own keeper, Piet Schrijvers, forcing him off injured. Reeling from such a double blow, Holland were fortunate not to go further behind before half-time as the Azzurri, with Paolo Rossi a constant threat, tormented them time and again. Then, five minutes after the break and totally against the run of play, Brandts made up for his earlier error with interest, smashing a loose ball into the top corner from 25 yards. Still, it was Italy doing all the running and Holland hanging on. But with time running out, Arie Haan produced another wonder strike from extreme range, this one even further out than against Germany; letting fly from almost 45 yards out wide on the left, the ball arrowed past the groping Dino Zoff and into the top corner. With that, Italy were eliminated, though there was no doubt they had been the better team not only in the match but the tournament as a whole. However, it would be Holland who would play in the final, their second in succession.

In Group B, **Brazil** faced **Poland** in Mendoza. Starting strongly, the South Americans took an early lead when right-back Nelinho powered home a free-kick awarded after a strong run from Gil had been halted on the edge of the box. Poland were not about to give up, however, Kazimierz Deyna shooting just wide before they did manage an equaliser on the stroke of half-time. Antoni Szymanowski and Zbigniew Boniek combined superbly down the right before the loose ball eventually fell for the ever-alert Grzegorz Lato to stab home. Brazil were not to be deterred, however. Toninho's cross from the left saw Mendonca crash a rasping shot off the post and the lurking Roberto Dinamite prodded in the rebound. Still the South Americans attacked. Mendonca and Gil both struck the woodwork in quick succession before Dirceu did the same from 25 yards, this time Roberto again in the right place to turn in the rebound. The Poles rallied late on with Szarmach, Lubanski, Deyna, Gorgon and Boniek all failing to score from fine opportunities, but they were far from disgraced. Brazil, meanwhile, continued to improve. They would now await the outcome of Argentina's clash with Peru but there was no doubt the Selecao were in pole position to reach the final.

Again given the highly unfair benefit of playing their match after their opponents, thereby knowing exactly what result was needed to progress, **Argentina** took on **Peru** in Rosario knowing that only the improbable scenario of victory by four goals or more would take them to the final. This seemed unlikely, especially after they survived an early scare when Peru winger Juan Jose Munante raced through the defence and beat keeper Fillol only for his shot to come back off the inside of the far post. As it happened, however, this was as close as Peru came to putting up a fight against the hosts as from then on they fell apart embarrassingly. The rout started after 21 minutes when Mario Kempes burst into the box and slotted calmly past Ramon Quiroga. Before half-time it was 2-0, left-back Alberto Tarantini leaping to head in Daniel Bertoni's corner. Just five minutes into the second half Argentina had the four goals required for qualification, Kempes combining well with centre forward Leopoldo Luque to slot in the third before Luque headed home Daniel Passarella's ball from point blank range. The massacre didn't end there, Oscar Ortiz pulling one back across the face for substitute Rene Houseman to roll in and Luque sliding a shot past Quiroga five minutes later. Peru had been humiliated and Argentina had reached only their second ever World Cup final, after losing to Uruguay way back in 1930. There were suspicions, however, that the Peruvians had been bribed to play so poorly and many, particularly the Brazilians, eliminated without losing a single game, were less than happy with the manner of the hosts' progression.

Only at the World Cup

It is believed by many that Argentina's fascist government bribed Peru to lose heavily to allow the hosts to reach the final at the expense of Brazil. Nothing could be proved, however, but, together with dubious refereeing decisions in previous games, it meant Argentina's run to the final was somewhat tainted.

Second Round results

Group A

West Germany 0-0 Italy
14/06/78 – Buenos Aires (Monumental)
West Germany: Maier, Vogts (c), Russmann, Dietz, Zimmermann (Konopa), Kaltz, Bonhof, Flohe (Beer), Rummenigge, Fischer, Holzenbein
Italy: Zoff (c), Gentile, Bellugi, Scirea, Cabrini, Benetti, Tardelli, Antognoni (Zaccarelli), Causio, Rossi, Bettega
Referee: Maksimovic (Yugoslavia)

Holland 5-1 Austria
14/06/78 – Cordoba (Estadio Cordoba)
Holland: Schrijvers, Brandts (Van Kraay), Wildschut, Krol (c), Poortvliet, Jansen, Haan, W Van de Kerkhof, R Van de Kerkhof (Schoenaker), Rep, Rensenbrink
Goals: Brandts 6, Rensenbrink pen 35, Rep 36, 53, W Van de Kerkhof 82
Austria: Koncilia, Sara (c), Pezzey, Obermayer, Breitenberger, Hickersberger, Prohaska, Krieger, Jara, Krankl, Kreuz
Goals: Obermayer 79
Referee: Gordon (Scotland)

Italy 1-0 Austria
18/06/78 – Buenos Aires (Monumental)
Italy: Zoff (c), Gentile, Bellugi (Cuccureddu), Scirea, Cabrini, Benetti, Tardelli, Zaccarelli, Causio, Rossi, Bettega (Graziani)
Goals: Rossi 14
Austria: Koncilia, Sara (c), Pezzey, Obermayer, Strasser, Hickersberger, Prohaska, Krieger, Schachner (Pirkner), Krankl, Kreuz
Referee: Rion (Belgium)

West Germany 2-2 Holland
18/06/78 – Cordoba (Estadio Cordoba)
West Germany: Maier, Vogts (c), Russmann, Dietz, Kaltz, Bonhof, Beer, Rummenigge, Abramczik, Holzenbein, D Muller
Goals: Abramczik 3, D Muller 70
Holland: Schrijvers, Brandts, Wildschut (Nanninga), Krol (c), Poortvliet, Jansen, Haan, W Van de Kerkhof, R Van de Kerkhof, Rep, Rensenbrink
Goals: Haan 27, R Van de Kerkhof 84
Sent off: Nanninga 88
Referee: Barreto (Uruguay)

Austria 3-2 West Germany
21/06/78 – Cordoba (Estadio Cordoba)
Austria: Koncilia, Sara (c), Pezzey, Obermayer, Strasser, Hickersberger, Prohaska, Krieger, Schachner (Oberacher), Krankl, Kreuz
Goals: Vogts (og) 59, Krankl 66, 87
West Germany: Maier, Vogts (c), Russmann, Dietz, Kaltz, Bonhof, Beer (H Muller), Rummenigge, Abramczik, Holzenbein, D Muller (Fischer)
Goals: Rummenigge 19, Holzenbein 72
Referee: Klein (Israel)

Holland 2-1 Italy
21/06/78 – Buenos Aires (Monumental)
Holland: Schrijvers (Jongbloed), Brandts, Krol (c), Poortvliet, Jansen, Neeskens, Haan, W Van de Kerkhof, R Van de Kerkhof, Rep (Van Kraay), Rensenbrink
Goals: Brandts 50, Haan 75
Italy: Zoff (c), Gentile, Cuccureddu, Scirea, Cabrini, Benetti (Graziani), Tardelli, Zaccarelli, Causio (C Sala), Rossi, Bettega
Goals: Brandts (og) 18
Referee: Martinez (Spain)

	Pld	W	D	L	GF	GA	Pts
Holland	3	2	1	0	9	4	5
Italy	3	1	1	1	2	2	3
West Germany	3	0	2	1	4	5	2
Austria	3	1	0	2	4	8	2

Holland qualified for final, Italy to third-place play-off.

Group B

Brazil 3-0 Peru
14/06/78 – Mendoza (Ciudad de Mendoza)
Brazil: Leao (c), Toninho, Amaral, Oscar, Rodrigues Neto, Cerezo (Chicao), Batista, Dirceu, Gil (Zico), Mendonca, Roberto Dinamite
Goals: Dirceu 15, 28, Zico pen 73
Peru: Quiroga, Duarte, Chumpitaz (c), Diaz (Navarro), Manzo, Cueto, Velasquez, Cubillas, Munante, La Rosa, Oblitas (P Rojas)
Referee: Rainea (Romania)

Argentina 2-0 Poland
14/06/78 – Rosario (Gigante de Arroyito)
Argentina: Fillol, Olguin, L Galvan, Passarella (c), Tarantini, Ardiles, Gallego, Valencia (Villa), Houseman (Ortiz), Kempes, Bertoni
Goals: Kempes 16, 71
Poland: Tomaszewski, Szymanowski, Kasperczak, Zmuda, Maculewicz, Nawalka, Deyna (c), Masztaler (Mazur), Boniek, Lato, Szarmach
Referee: Eriksson (Sweden)

Poland 1-0 Peru
18/06/78 – Mendoza (Ciudad de Mendoza)
Poland: Kukla, Szymanowski, Gorgon, Zmuda, Maculewicz, Nawalka, Deyna (c), Masztaler (Kasperczak), Boniek (Lubanski), Lato, Szarmach
Goals: Szarmach 65
Peru: Quiroga, Duarte, Chumpitaz (c), Navarro, Manzo, Cueto, Quesada, Cubillas, Munante (P Rojas), La Rosa (Sotil), Oblitas
Referee: Partridge (England)

Argentina 0-0 Brazil
18/06/78 – Rosario (Gigante de Arroyito)
Argentina: Fillol, Olguin, L Galvan, Passarella (c), Tarantini, Ardiles (Villa), Gallego, Kempes, Bertoni, Luque, Ortiz (Alonso)
Brazil: Leao (c), Toninho, Amaral, Oscar, Rodrigues Neto (Edinho), Chicao, Batista, Dirceu, Gil, Mendonca (Zico), Roberto Dinamite
Referee: Palotai (Hungary)

Brazil 3-1 Poland
21/06/78 – Mendoza (Ciudad de Mendoza)
Brazil: Leao (c), Nelinho, Amaral, Oscar, Toninho, Cerezo (Rivelino), Batista, Dirceu, Zico (Mendonca), Gil, Roberto Dinamite
Goals: Nelinho 13, Roberto Dinamite 57, 63
Poland: Kukla, Szymanowski, Gorgon, Zmuda, Maculewicz, Nawalka, Kasperczak (Lubanski), Deyna (c), Boniek, Lato, Szarmach
Goals: Lato 45
Referee: Silvagno (Chile)

Argentina 6-0 Peru
21/06/78 – Rosario (Gigante de Arroyito)
Argentina: Fillol, Olguin, L Galvan, Passarella (c), Tarantini, Larrosa, Gallego (Oviedo), Kempes, Bertoni (Houseman), Luque, Ortiz
Goals: Kempes 21, 46, Tarantini 43, Luque 50, 72, Houseman 67
Peru: Quiroga, Duarte, Chumpitaz (c), R Rojas, Manzo, Cueto, Velasquez (Gorriti), Quesada, Cubillas, Munante, Oblitas
Referee: Wurtz (France)

	Pld	W	D	L	GF	GA	Pts
Argentina	3	2	1	0	8	0	5
Brazil	3	2	1	0	6	1	5
Poland	3	1	0	2	2	5	2
Peru	3	0	0	3	0	10	0

Argentina qualified for final, Brazil to third-place play-off.

World Cup Great – Kazimierz Deyna (Poland)

Poland exploded onto the global footballing stage as one of the world's best sides in the 1970s with a terrific run of results in the World Cup and the Olympic Games. This great side had many exceptional players but none were more talented or more important to the team's success than the captain and playmaker Kazimierz Deyna. Without his cool, calm leadership, incredible vision and passing skills and deadly accurate shooting the Poles would have been half the team they were.

Deyna first made his name at top Polish club Legia Warsaw, the side he joined in 1966. His mature and able performances quickly caught the eye of the national team and he made his debut aged 20 in 1968. By this time Deyna had already established himself as his club's key player, helping them to back-to-back titles at the turn of the decade. It was at the Munich Olympics in 1972, however, that Deyna really came to the attention of the world as he led Poland to an unexpected gold medal, orchestrating a highly talented team from deep while supplying a deadly goalscoring touch. Indeed, the nine goals he scored in the tournament were enough for him to finish top scorer. Two of those goals came in the final against Hungary, lifting his side back from a goal down to triumph gloriously.

Understandably after such performances, Poland were highly thought of by the time they reached their first World Cup in 36 years with the 1974 edition in West Germany. Deyna was the team's captain and star player as the Poles claimed an improbable third-place finish, which included glorious victories over the likes of Argentina, Italy and Yugoslavia. The team's general and key provider, Deyna was honoured by finishing third in the voting for the prestigious European Footballer of the Year award that season.

Deyna and Poland would further enhance their names at the 1976 Olympics and 1978 World Cup, claiming the silver medal in the former and topping a group including reigning champions West Germany in the latter before eventually being edged out by Brazil and Argentina in the second phase. Deyna excelled in both competitions but this was the end of his international career, leaving the team with a superb record of 97 caps and 41 goals.

The end of the 1978 World Cup also marked the end of Deyna's time at Legia Warsaw as he departed for Manchester City in England, where he would remain for three years. However, Deyna was rarely able to recapture his form of old in his new surroundings, not helped by persistent injuries, and he left for the North American Soccer League in 1981, where he would see out his career. Sadly, Deyna would have little time after his retirement to reflect on his exceptional career: he died in a car crash in 1989 at the age of just 41.

Nowadays the goalscoring feats of team mates Grzegorz Lato and Zbigniew Boniek might make them more famous, at least outside Poland, but few who watched him play would dispute that Kazimierz Deyna was Poland's greatest player in their golden generation of the 1970s and early 80s. Blessed with supremely accurate passing, an unrivalled ability to pull the strings from deep and a vicious shot from range, Deyna was the man who made an exceptionally talented side tick. Few would question that he ranks amongst the world's very greatest playmakers.

Third-place Play-off

Only at the World Cup

Brazil full-back Nelinho scored an unrepeatable goal against Italy. Taking a shot from way out on the right touchline, Nelinho struck the ball viciously with the outside of his boot, causing it to swerve outrageously back in and around the helpless keeper to fly into the top corner.

Many World Cup third-place play-offs in the past have been lamentably dull affairs devoid of passion. This match, however, between probably the two most talented sides in the whole competition in **Italy** and **Brazil**, was an exceptional game from start to finish. Both sides fielded strong line-ups and both, despite the heartache of missing out on the final, seemed desperate for the consolation prize of the bronze medal. The Europeans were far the quicker out of the blocks and utterly dominated the first period, running Brazil ragged. Playmakers Giancarlo Antognoni and Franco Causio were both exceptional, Antognoni stinging the palms of keeper Leao early on before testing the strength of his crossbar with a ferocious shot. Eventually, the Azzurri achieved the breakthrough they deserved, Paolo Rossi floating over a teasing cross to the far post for the arriving Causio to head in. Italy should have been further ahead at the break, Causio and Rossi both hitting the woodwork as Brazil desperately clung on. However, a goal out of nowhere midway through the second half utterly changed the complexion of the game. The scorer was Brazil right-back Nelinho and the goal was one of the greatest ever at a World Cup. Receiving the ball out on the right touchline, Nelinho showed off the sort of flair that only Brazilians possess by going for goal and he was rewarded as his perfect swinging shot left Dino Zoff with absolutely no chance as it arrowed into the top far corner. Suddenly it was the South Americans who were pouring forward in numbers and when Dirceu cracked in Mendonca's lay-off from the edge of the area for another outstanding goal, Italy were behind. Despite their domination, which would also see Roberto Bettega head a Causio free-kick against the bar before the finish, they had lost narrowly, denied by the glorious shooting of their opponents. Brazil had some small measure of consolation for missing out on the final in controversial circumstances. The fear, however, was that there was little chance that Argentina and Holland could produce such a high-quality spectacle in the final match itself.

Third-place Play-off result

Italy 1-2 Brazil
24/06/78 – Buenos Aires (Monumental)
Italy: Zoff (c), Gentile, Cuccureddu, Scirea, Maldera, Cabrini, P Sala, Antognoni (C Sala), Causio, Rossi, Bettega
Goals: Causio 38
Brazil: Leao (c), Nelinho, Amaral, Oscar, Rodrigues Neto, Cerezo (Rivelino), Batista, Dirceu, Gil (Reinaldo), Mendonca, Roberto Dinamite
Goals: Nelinho 64, Dirceu 72
Referee: Klein (Israel)

Brazil claimed third place.

World Cup Final

The final took place at River Plate's Estadio Monumental in Buenos Aires and the partisan crowd awaited the arrival of the home team **Argentina** with great excitement. Both they and **Holland**, however, were made to wait a good five minutes after the Dutch had taken the field before Cesar Menotti's team finally made it onto the pitch but when they did the reception was deafening. Ticker tape poured down from the stands and flooded the pitch in an incredible display of passion from a country fanatical about football. The Argentines' questionable pre-game tactics, however, weren't to stop at making the Dutch wait as they then complained about a cast on Rene Van de Kerkhof's arm. The Dutch winger had played with his arm bandaged for several games already without issue but Italian referee Sergio Gonella scandalously seemed to uphold the hosts' protests. It briefly appeared that there would be no final after all as the Dutch threatened to walk off the field but eventually an extra bandage was placed round Van de Kerkhof's hand and the game could finally get underway, even though the ticker tape covering the pitch made play difficult for both sides. Both teams had early opportunities, Johnny Rep for Holland and Daniel Passarella for Argentina twice coming close but keepers Ubaldo Fillol and Jan Jongbloed not in the mood to be beaten so early on. Then Leopoldo Luque found Mario Kempes on the edge of the area. The Valencia man's first touch was superb, taking him clear of his marker and through on goal. Jongbloed came rushing out but Kempes coolly slipped the ball under him to give the hosts the lead to the joy of the 71,000 in the crowd. Holland, largely the better side, were undeterred and almost equalised at the end of the half when Rob Rensenbrink's shot from close range was superbly blocked by Fillol.

> ## Only at the World Cup
>
> Argentina's fans created an incredible atmosphere for the final, including welcoming their team with a vast ticker tape reception. However, the upshot of this was that both sides were forced to play on a surface now covered with litter.

> ## Only at the World Cup
>
> The 1978 World Cup final was almost over before it started as Holland threatened to walk off the pitch after Argentina had made them wait a full five minutes before taking the field and then, with the referee's backing, complained about a bandage on Rene Van de Kerkhof's arm.

On the hour, coach Ernst Happel threw on tall striker Dick Nanninga, hoping to exploit the South Americans' lack of height at the back. The move worked to perfection eight minutes from time when Rene Van de Kerkhof crossed from the right and Nanninga towered above the Argentine defence to head in the leveller. Now it was Holland who were in the ascendancy and Rensenbrink should have won it in the dying seconds of normal time but his shot came back off the post. For the first time since 1966, the final would be going to extra time. Argentina's own substitute, winger Rene Houseman, caused problems to tired legs as the Dutch were forced on the defensive but it was to be the inspired Kempes who would become his country's hero. In the final minute of the first period of extra time the forward received the ball running into the area, weaved his way through the challenges of two defenders and shot as Jongbloed came bursting out to meet him. The keeper blocked the

shot but luck was clearly with Kempes that day as the rebound fell straight to him and he was just able to slide the ball in before the scrambling defence could deny him. There was pandemonium in the stands as the stadium celebrated wildly, realising this was the moment that would see Argentina crowned world champions for the first time. So it proved as, for the final 15 minutes, Holland fell apart. Sensing their chances slipping away, they resorted to violence in what had already been a horrendously brutal encounter. Still, it was not enough to prevent one more moment of Argentinean glory. Inevitably it was the majestic Kempes who was at the centre of it, his strong run into the box eventually halted but the loose ball falling for winger Daniel Bertoni to stab home. Argentina were champions, deserving winners of the game even if their run to the final had been filled with controversy. Holland, meanwhile, were heartbroken once again and the manner of their defeat, particularly the way the match had begun, infuriated them.

World Cup Final result

Holland 1-3 Argentina (aet)
25/06/78 – Buenos Aires (Monumental)
Holland: Jongbloed, Brandts, Krol (c), Poortvliet, Jansen (Suurbier), Neeskens, Haan, W Van de Kerkhof, R Van de Kerkhof, Rep (Nanninga), Rensenbrink
Goals: Nanninga 82
Argentina: Fillol, Olguin, L Galvan, Passarella (c), Tarantini, Ardiles (Larrosa), Gallego, Kempes, Bertoni, Luque, Ortiz (Houseman)
Goals: Kempes 38, 105, Bertoni 116
Referee: Gonella (Italy)

Argentina won the 1978 World Cup.

Tournament awards

Golden Boot: Mario Kempes (Argentina) – 6 goals
(Runners-up: Teofilo Cubillas (Peru)/Rob Rensenbrink (Holland) – 5)

Best Player: Mario Kempes (Argentina)

Best Goal: Nelinho (Brazil) – No other World Cup ever has had more worthy contenders for this position than 1978, with a host of exceptional goals scored. However, right-back Nelinho scored arguably the pick of the bunch against Italy, shooting from the right by-line with such outrageous swerve that the ball swung back in past Zoff and into the top corner.

Star XI:
Goalkeeper – Ubaldo Fillol (Argentina)
Defenders – Jorge Olguin (Argentina), Ruud Krol (Holland), Daniel Passarella (Argentina), Antonio Cabrini (Italy)
Midfielders – Dirceu (Brazil), Teofilo Cubillas (Peru), Mario Kempes (Argentina)
Forwards – Paolo Rossi (Italy), Hans Krankl (Austria), Rob Rensenbrink (Holland)

World Cup Great – Johan Neeskens (Holland)

The great Holland side of the 1970s is generally, and rightly, remembered as one of the greatest attacking sides of all time. However, the policy of "Total Football" also placed great emphasis on defence. While Johan Cruyff was strutting his stuff and causing his opponents problems, Johan Neeskens was busying himself winning the ball for his maestro. Had Neeskens not been in the team, Holland would have been all bark and no bite.

Neeskens initially started out as a defender at local side RCH before impressing enough to be signed by top club Ajax as a teenager in 1970, winning his first international cap that same year. Playing at right-back, Neeskens helped his new club win the European Cup in 1971. However, it was when coach Rinus Michels had the bright idea of playing the tigerish Neeskens in central midfield that his career really took off. His incredible stamina, pace, aerial ability and crunching strength in the tackle made him an awe-inspiring holding midfielder and the rock upon which Ajax's further two European Cup wins in the following seasons were built. Charged with keeping tabs on the opposition's playmaker, Neeskens was one of the first players to quickly close down his opponents, forcing them into misplaced passes by cutting down their time on the ball. However, he was far more than just a hatchet man. The "Total Football" style of which he was such an important component for Ajax and Holland demanded all-round ability and Neeskens was composed in possession, regularly starting his team's attacks by winning the ball and feeding the front runners, while he also possessed a potent goal threat himself, including a formidable long-range shot.

Holland's exceptional displays in the 1974 World Cup would not have been possible without Neeskens. The midfielder, one of the youngest players in the squad, was in irresistible form, putting in phenomenal all-round performances in midfield, covering when his team mates attacked, winning the ball for them and indeed finishing as his team's top scorer with five goals. One of these was a penalty to give Holland the lead in the final. Sadly for Neeskens and his team, however, they would go on to lose the match 2-1 to their bitter rivals West Germany.

Neeskens joined Michels and Cruyff at Barcelona in 1974, starring there for five years and becoming a firm fan favourite for his ability and heart-on-sleeve commitment. During this period he would again star at the World Cup in 1978. Although not quite as dominant as in Germany, Neeskens was still the key ball-winner in the midfield and a crucial component of the team. He was instrumental in Holland reaching the final for the second successive time, though again he could do nothing to prevent his side losing once more to the hosts, this time Argentina, in a cynical and violent match not helped by poor refereeing.

This would mark the end of Neesken's career at the very top. The following year he would leave Barcelona for the North American Soccer League and his final match for Holland came in 1981, as he failed to prevent a side in transition from slipping out of the race to qualify for the 1982 World Cup. Still, his record of 17 goals in 49 internationals from a largely defensive position was hugely impressive. Neeskens saw out the twilight years of his career in Switzerland, eventually retiring in 1991.

Often overlooked in favour of his more attacking team mates Cruyff and Rob Rensenbrink, in reality Neeskens was probably Holland's most irreplacable player. Without his ability and passion in midfield, all Holland's creative talent would have been starved of the ball they craved. A true footballing all-rounder, Neesken's great versatility combined with his exceptional ability means he vies with Germany's Lothar Matthaus for the title of the greatest ever defensive midfielder.

World Cup Great – Roberto Rivelino (Brazil)

Few figures in 1970s world football were as instantly identifiable as great Brazil midfielder Roberto Rivelino. With his bristling moustache and eccentric style on the pitch, he stood out from his team mates but these were not the only qualities that got him noticed. Famous for his thunderous shooting, exceptional passing and flair, Rivelino was one of the brightest stars even in a Brazil team considered by many to be the greatest ever.

The young Rivelino first came to prominence at Sao Paulo giants Corinthians, making his debut for the first team as a 19-year-old in 1965. Instantly catching the eye with his composed and elegant displays in the midfield, he was selected to make his first start for Brazil that same year, although unlike several other youngsters he was overlooked for the 1966 World Cup, in which his country suffered a shock first-round exit. Nevertheless, his exceptional performances for Corinthians soon thrust him to the forefront of Brazil's plans.

Going into the 1970 World Cup in Mexico, Brazil had a far from settled line-up. Mario Zagallo was brought in as coach in an effort to find the right balance to the team. One of his first and most important moves was to bring Rivelino into the side at the expense of left winger Paulo Cesar. Initially this move was questioned, considering at this point Rivelino was generally considered a central midfielder. However, Zagallo was eager for both him and playmaker Gerson to play in the same side to increase Brazil's creativity. Therefore he decided to use Rivelino on the left of a midfield trio, encouraging him also to push up at times to operate almost as a left winger. For Rivelino this was a new position but the young midfielder adapted exceptionally. He was one of the stars of the tournament as Brazil's glittering attacking side swept all before them to take the title. Rivelino scored three goals in the tournament, all thunderous shots as was his trademark.

By the time of the 1974 World Cup, most of Brazil's stars had retired, leaving the 28-year-old Rivelino as his side's main man. Although Brazil were a shadow of their former selves Rivelino was still a star, again notching three goals, including another deadly powerful and accurate free-kick, to help Brazil to fourth. That season he left Corinthians for Fluminense, becoming a fan favourite there just as he had been in Sao Paulo and ensuring with his good form he would make it to the 1978 World Cup, the only member of the 1970 vintage still in the squad. Sadly for Rivelino, he would mainly be a substitute at the tournament as age caught up with him and he struggled with his best form. Still, he left the international stage with 92 caps and 26 goals. In the same year he would also leave Brazil for Saudi Arabia, playing out the final years of his career at Al Hilal.

Rivelino was always a hugely popular player in Brazil and a large part of this was due to the style of his play on the pitch. Always composed on the field, he was noticeable for his long raking passes but most of all for his exceptionally powerful shooting. When Rivelino had the ball at his feet all the crowd were expecting a thunderbolt from distance and Rivelino scored many such goals in his career, particularly from free-kicks, succeeding Didi as the master of the "Banana Shot". Rivelino was also blessed with unique flair and ability to beat his man, inventing a move known as the "Elastico" whereby he would drag the ball one way with his foot before knocking it the other way in a flash. Many Brazilians since have copied him but Rivelino will always be the master of the move. Plenty of stories still abound, some no doubt false, of the outrageous tricks Rivelino would attempt on the pitch. One particularly famous one credits him with scoring a goal straight from the opening kick-off, lobbing the keeper while he was deep in prayer (this incredible story also states that the keeper's brother, incensed by the goal, ran onto the pitch with a revolver in his hand and shot the ball six times!). There is no doubt, however, that Rivelino was a player blessed with a rare gift for thinking and innovating on his feet. This added to his incredible footballing skill to make him the sort of footballing genius only Brazil could ever produce.

Overall, much of the football on display at the 1978 World Cup had been of the highest quality, certainly putting to shame the drab encounters typical of the previous tournament. Great goals had flowed in abundance, while several highly talented and closely matched teams had battled it out for the trophy. The incredible passion of the home fans too had been a massive positive and no-one would forget the rapturous reception given to the hosts as they took to the field for the final itself.

However, the sense remained that Argentina had been fortunate to lift the trophy. Undoubtedly a talented team and one of the best sides in the tournament, nevertheless they had at times been scandalously favoured by referees. This is generally true of all hosts but the fact that so much foul play went unpunished left something of a bitter taste in the mouth. Worse still, the advantage of playing all their games after their group rivals, the controversy surrounding the allegedly fixed Peru match and their pre-game antics in the final all contributed to somewhat devalue what had otherwise been an exceptional achievement for a team who had never before won the trophy. At least the likes of Kempes, Luque and Passarella had performed outstandingly on the pitch and were amongst the competition's foremost stars.

Holland again had suffered the agony of defeat in a final and were left to rue the absence of the inspirational Cruyff. Nevertheless, a team in decline had probably punched above their weight to reach the competition's climax and they were indebted to the fine performances of Rob Rensenbrink, who stepped out of Cruyff's shadow to be his side's main man. If only his shot in the dying minutes of normal time had gone in rather than hit the post it might all have been so different. As it was, the controversial manner of that final defeat and all the gamesmanship surrounding it infuriated the Dutch so much that they boycotted the post-match ceremonies in protest.

For Brazil and Italy, meanwhile, the agony was almost as great. Clearly the tournament's best two teams, it was a shame their meeting occurred in the third-place play-off rather than the final. Both were exceptional throughout, with Brazil not losing a single match and the Italians being the only side to (deservedly) beat Argentina. The fact that both were young sides at least boded well for their chances next time around.

As for the rest of the field, Poland again showed their quality while Austria sprung a real surprise in beating West Germany, who ultimately were found lacking the quality they had possessed four years earlier. Peru too had shone at times, though their exceptional performances in the first round were somewhat devalued by their shambolic displays in the second phase. Then there was Scotland, victors over Holland but unable to beat Iran and Peru. It was a shame for the competition that one of its most gifted sides fell in the first round and the blame could firmly be laid at the feet of coach Ally MacLeod, whose foolish pre-tournament comments had burdened his team with expectation they were not capable of dealing with. Still, at least against the Dutch they had lit up the tournament and they, like many others, could reflect on what was largely an engrossing and exciting competition. Everyone hoped that Spain 1982 would be no different.

131

Printed in Great Britain
by Amazon